Who Needs SYSTEMS FOR SUCCESS?

Interior Designers working independently out of their homes

Never apologize or feel "small" working out of your home. It can be a smart decision economically. This book will motivate and inspire you to become more professional and not feel so alone.

Experienced Designers

This book offers motivational techniques and high energy for those who have been practicing interior design for many years. Interior design is a high turnover career. To keep motivated and enthused means to keep reading and seeking applicable input.

Interior Design or Design Related Firms

Halverson has worked for others, managed staffs of over 30 designers and had her own design studio. The material enclosed was created to help her staff grow as well as her business. This is an ideal book to use for staff meetings and workshops.

Senior Interior Design students

This book is about the real world of interior design. If you intend to support yourself financially, this book will show you how. It is 15 years of on-the-job experience, practical day to day operational systems, easy to implement. **Systems for Success** is a necessity for all designers!

Major firms with salespersons servicing interior designers

As a national spokesperson and columnist for the interior design industry, Kate Halverson became aware how frustrated manufacturers representatives are with interior designers and their overall professionalism. **Systems For Success** is very similar in form and content to operating manuals major franchise firms are giving to licensees who pay $ 15,000-$40,000 for franchise opportunities. What a great gift or workshop tool this book could be for you and the designers you service.

SYSTEMS FOR SUCCESS

A "How-to Manual"
For
Today's Interior Designer

by
Kate Halverson

Weston Communications

Production Director: Aimee Richcreek
Cover Design: Jeremy Gale
Edited by: Craig Halverson & Margaret Labash Young

H G F E D C B

Library of Congress Cataloging-in-Publication Data
Halverson, Kate.
Systems For Success, A "How -To" Manual For Today's Interior Designer".
Includes Index
LC 89-51681
ISBN 0-9623401-1-1

Weston Communications
10280 County Road 18
Eden Prairie, MN 55347
612/941-3090

Dedication

This book is dedicated to the interior design industry. It was written mainly out of concern for fellow designers. What appears to be a highly glamorous and creative profession, is a difficult profession in which to survive financially.

My hope is that **Systems For Success** will offer valuable advice to those dedicated to the field of interior design.

Kate Halverson

Contents

Contents

Introduction

Congratulations on your commitment to be an interior designer. Although it's not an easy profession, it can be very rewarding, offering great opportunities in sales and creative design.

BE AWARE

1. Design expertise comes from continual exposure and accumulated experience.
2. Interior design demands a tremendous amount of ongoing research.
3. To be successful you can no longer be idealistic. Ideal projects and clients are not reality.
4. Discipline and dedication to your profession are essential to design success and monetary rewards.
5. Interior design demands high energy, stamina and passion. It is a very emotional business with long days and continual pressures.
6. You must really enjoy people. Success depends on your social networking.
7. To succeed you must stay organized. Attending to countless details can make or break you!

and finally. . . . .

8. Successful designers, live, eat and breathe design - I do, and I love it even after 15 years!

If you know the above as truth, this book will provide you with a simplistic, desktop approach to polish your systems and your professionalism. It has been designed and written to become an ongoing Interior Design Notebook. Keep it handy near or on your desktop. Take it with you to upcoming design seminars and workshops. Write in it and use it. Use the index. If you shelve it, you will forget it!

I've been asked: Who should buy this book?

1. **Interior Designers** working independently out of their homes

   Never apologize or feel "small" working out of your home. It can be a smart decision economically. This book will help to motivate and inspire you to become more professional and not feel so alone.

2. **Interior Design or Design Related Firms**   (Drapery Workrooms, Furniture Stores, Flooring Stores, and Wallcovering Stores)

   I have worked for others, managed staffs of over 30 designers and had my own design studio. The material enclosed was created to help my staff grow as well as my business. This is an ideal book to use for staff meetings and workshops.

3. Major firms with **salespersons** servicing interior designers. (Drapery and Bedspread Manufacturers, Furniture Manufacturers, Window Treatment Manufacturers, Design Showrooms)

   As a national spokesperson and columnist for the interior design industry, I've become aware how frustrated manufacturers representatives are with interior designers and their overall professionalism. **Systems For Success** is very similar in form and content to operating manuals major franchise firms are giving to licensees who pay $ 15,000-$40,000 for franchise opportunities. What a great gift or workshop tool this book could be for you and the designers you service.

4. **Senior interior design students**
   This book is about the real world of interior design. If you intend to support yourself financially, this book is a bargain. It is 15 years of on-the-job experience, practical day - to - day operational systems, easy to

implement. It is a unique book.

Finally, **Systems For Success** is not intended to be read and absorbed in a few sittings. It is a handbook. That means it is intended to be an ongoing "hands-on" book.

It has been said that it takes 21 days to change a habit. My suggestion is that you focus each week on something new. Focus - Focus - Focus for one week on changing one particular habit. Move on to another area the next week. Don't forget to work on week one's problem continually.

Example:

Week 1 - Focus on Networking (new)
Week 2 - Focus on Problem Solving (new)
     Focus on Networking (old)
Week 3 - Focus on Professionalism (new)
     Focus on Problem Solving (old)
     Focus on Networking (old)
Week 4 - By now you've had 21 days of networking
     focus - you should be getting better. It
     should be a new habit.

If you go back to an old habit, you'll need to go back to refocusing on changing it. Work, yes, but so is staying in business and making a living.

"The common denominator for success is work. Without work, man loses his vision, his confidence and his determination to achieve."

      John D. Rockefeller

I truly care about our profession. We have much work to do to bring credibility to the field of interior design. You can be an asset to our profession. My hope is that **Systems For Success** will be a major step in achieving your successes!

Best Wishes

KMH

Corporate Philosophy

Whether you are a one person studio or part of a larger design group, having a corporate philosophy or mission statement is important. When I started my own business as a one person studio with an answering machine, I still had a corporate philosophy. I typed my first Business Plan and showed it to my banker. (I wasn't even going to borrow money then.)

The purpose of your mission statement is to keep you on target. Take time this month to develop your mission statement for the coming year. I've written my mission statement several times over the years.

My mission statement is:

Touch of Class Interiors, Ltd. seeks to provide professional, creative design services and products for both residential and commercial clients at an affordable price. These services will be provided while retaining a professional image, obtaining a manageable growth rate and continued profitability. Touch of Class Interiors, Ltd. will employ only efficient professionals enhancing its reputation as one of the area's prime design resource centers.

Subject to change whenever you choose to revise your professional course.

Quality Assurance

With alternative options available to the public (catalog purchasing, discount outlets, toll-free number systems, and large mass marketing department stores), designers are searching for systems to assist them in making a living in the interior design business.

Design excellence and price are not the only determining factors for interior design services. Complete full servicing opportunities and adequate collection and business data are equally important.

A quality assurance system provides for check points to assist every designer in sharpening skills to take clients through the total client full-service process.

This manual has been designed and written to assist you in developing your own personal "Quality Assurance" program, whether you are a small design firm of one or part of a larger organization. If you are to survive professionally, you must begin today to develop a quality assurance program. **To be a professional, a designer needs to have: systems, skills, and discipline. If this manual is adhered to, you will have all three. You will be a true professional, something only 10% of all salespeople really are.**

Designer's Code of Ethics

1.   Always be honest.

2.   Treat clients like "royalty".

3.   Service! Service! Service! ...but don't be used!

4.   Be professional, at all times.

5.   Keep a sense of humor when things get "heavy".

6.   Take care of your clients - remember their joys
     and sorrows. Send cards and flowers.

7.   Be prepared...24 hours ahead of time!

8.   Be goal-oriented...know your direction...know your
     plan.

9.   Show initiative...be a pre-thinker! This applies to
     pre-planning to prevent unforeseen problems.
     (We call this our PPP Program - Preplan to
     Prevent Problems!)

10. Remember manners - "Thank You" and "I'm
     Sorry".

System 1: *Success*

Success

The first memory I have of the word 'success' was when a very successful stockbrocker told me of his rules of thumb. Every morning as he drove to work, he thought about what he had done yesterday and his goal was to double his sales each day! He told of his first lean weeks of making sales of $100. Pretty soon it was $200 a week, then $400 and soon $800 a week. I'm sure that today he is a millionaire several times over.

Those are great goals but after awhile, daily or weekly doubling gets pretty hard to do. Attitude is what really counts. The attitude of trying to do better tomorrow. Attitude is the key to both monetary and non-monetary successes. For me, non-monetary "successes" are equally important. They are reflected by:

- the balance in my life
- the relationships I have with people
- how I feel about myself

This book hopefully shows a balance between all of the above.

Designers need to remember that if they are truly going to be successful, they must train themselves to become professionals, and only then, will their design skills effectively assist them in making a living via their talents.

Being a Successful Designer

Over a 15 year time span, I have had the opportunity to work with many interior designers. Only a small percentage have become successful. Most of them have not begun to make an adequate living, much less support themselves or anyone else in the profession. If you fit the following, however, you have a good chance of making a living as an interior designer.

Profile:

1. Enthusiastic, uses positive approach in all aspects of life.
2. Excellent personal appearance.
3. Articulate - excellent communication skills.
4. Highly energetic.
5. Creative - helps clients "visualize" - yet understands that some of the time is spent "decorating" as opposed to designing.
6. Prefers quality merchandise and has a clear sense of good design. Understands that only about 20% of the business of interior design deals with the "prettys", the remaining 80% research, problem solving and paperwork.
7. Needs minimal supervision and enjoys researching and problem solving.
8. Likes to please self while pleasing others.
9. Understands that a designer must be a salesperson first.

The successful designer needs to be aware of the following pitfalls.

1. Poor use of time, generally means failure to make a living as a designer.
2. "Visiting" with clients meets social needs only, not financial needs.
3. Poor communications skills will affect sales.
4. Improper handling of paperwork will affect overall profit margins.

5. Making promises that can't be kept will create problems.

As Mary Knackstedt said in one of her columns, " *Most designers are not overnight successes, although it has happened. The majority of successes started early in their lives to study the processes that make design profitable. They continue to work on a day-to-day basis with these techniques, and with the right breaks, achieving a strong career. Long-term success always has a strong foundation in education, practical experience and discipline.*"

Success Starts with Making Goals

1. Goals should be made daily, weekly, monthly and yearly.
   A. **Daily Goals**
   These are a list of "musts" for the day. They have been prioritized in order of their importance. They are items which you know must be top priority. Categorize these items as #1 items. Any inter-staff memo or communication having a #1 on it tells a fellow staff member to: "get it done today"!

   Example of Daily Goals:
   Placing orders
   Returning phone calls
   Problem follow-up

   If a daily goal somehow does not get completed at the end of the day, it should be reassessed and placed in another day at the same or different priority level.

   Ask yourself the following questions on a daily basis:
   1) If I could do only one thing today, what would it be?
   2) If I could do only one thing today to be successful, what would it be?
   3) If I could do only two things today...etc.

   This will help you prioritize your daily, weekly and monthly lists better.

   B. **Weekly Goals:**
   Weekly planning is important in your calendar. It is recommended to plan your week with the following guidelines:

   1) 3 days for meeting with clients
   2) 1 day for prospecting and promotional or educational work
   3) 1 day for preparation/catch-up work

Placing appointments on a controlled calendar allows you to maximize your time. The important thing is to control and plan your weekly calendar by placing tasks on days when they are most convenient for you. You should be able to direct your activities to the geographical area you will be near for appointments and preparation tasks.

Suggestions:
- Think VIP clients first.
- Think potential sales opportunities first.
- Think daily priorities (top five) first.
- Think weekly goals first.

Example:

Monday
    AM...in for staff meeting
    phone calls/scheduling
    final prep work check for the week
    PM...client appointments...(in)

Tuesday
    AM...appointments...(out)
    PM...appointments...(in)

Wednesday
    long-range planning
    schedule a prospecting luncheon
    schedule promotional work
    meet with a manufacturer's representative
    explore a new showroom

Thursday
    appointments. . . . . downtown
    return samples

Friday
    preparation day
    AM...out of studio
    PM...in studio

It is strongly recommended that when you work with one particular client on a regular basis they have a fixed appointment time each week. This keeps things on track and leads to timely order placement.

C. **Monthly Goals**
These are tasks that you should complete by the month's end, if at all possible. Wednesday, or your long range planning day, is probably the only day you will have (if you've planned for it) to complete these tasks.

> *Examples:*
> * Meet four new good contacts (influential people) in the community.
> * Photograph completed job for use in portfolio.

D. **Quarterly and Yearly Goals**
Written goals are a must. You need to write three-month goal sheets regularly. Once again, if a goal is not completed, it just needs to be reassessed. The only point of writing goals is to identify which track you're really on. If you care about your profession, if it is a career, you will write three-month goals.

I have always written yearly goals. They have always been overly ambitious. I am not bothered by not achieving them at the end of the year. If they were not achieved, I need to reassess them and keep them on my next year's goal list if they still seem important. Do not be afraid of ambitious goals. You'll never achieve anything great if you don't have the direction to do so in the first place.

Sample Yearly Goals:
Reach $X00,000 sales

Weekly Goal Setting

1. **Daily/Weekly Goal Setting**
   A. Sales Goal of The Week:
      List the biggest client you hope to "Close" with:

      Approx. Amt of Sale_____
      Actual Sale_____

      Focus on your $5,000+ clients each week.

   B. Develop a Daily and Weekly Time Management Plan.

      Know where you're going this week. "Plan your work and work your plan."

      1) Identify your purpose before each presentation.
      2) Are all your activities geared toward promoting your overall business goals?
      3) Set definite timetables/attainable deadlines for projects.
      4) Do It - Work your plan!
      5) Review your goals frequently.

Monthly Goal Setting

1. **Goal Setting for the Month**
   A. Look at your past history...
      What have you averaged per month?

      _____
      Are you OK with that amount?
      Yes____ No_____
      Do you believe you can do better?
      Yes____ No_____
   B. What would you like to be selling per month?

      $_____minimum
      $_____average
      $_____maximum

   C. How are you going to make your quota?

      Week 1_____wallcovering orders
      _____furniture orders
      _____flooring orders
      _____window treatments
      _____fabric/upholstery
      _____lighting
      _____accessories/miscellaneous
      _____consultations

      Week 2-4 Same as above
      Are you spending the right amount of time on the
      right client?

   D. Think $X,000 a week in sales. (You might not
      make it, but you'll never make it if you don't think
      it!)

   F. Lay your month out:
      Week 1... Plan, prepare, schedule appointments
      Week 2 - 3...Present, prepare, present
      Week 4...Close, close, close

   G. If you don't have a better monthly plan, try this
      one!

Time is Money

We all know that time is one of our most valuable commodities, yet daily, one can easily become a . . . . . .

Time Waster
1. Doing things twice because it wasn't done right once!
2. Taking twice as long to do a job a true professional would do in half the time.
3. Just plain talking too much - - repeating what has already been said once!
4. Not listening effectively!

We often have no idea that we are losing valuable time. It is then we seem to moan the fact that there isn't enough time in the day.

I've also noted while observing the differences between a professional and an amateur that a professional will:

1. Explore options carefully.
2. Make decisions swiftly because they've done their homework.
3. Know what they're looking for - goals are clearly identified.

Any successful person knows that time is money. Truly successful people don't waste time. The following are: Ways in which achievers use their time.

1. **They plan. They set goals.** Accomplishment comes from achieving goals that have been set. Achievers spend their time making things happen instead of reacting to things that have already happened.

2. **They write things down.** Achievers set their priorities and give order to things, people and time, thereby achieving their dreams.

3. **They use their spare time to accomplish something.** They use time on the phone to do something with their hands - they listen to tapes in the car, read while waiting in line, etc.

4. **They don't allow themselves to be sidetracked.** When interrupted, they return to their original task.

5. **They don't procrastinate.** Motivation usually comes after the project is started, not before starting it.

6. **They delegate.**

7. **They organize** so that routine duties are done unconsciously.

8. **They follow through** to the end of a project as soon as possible.

The common factor in all these points is setting goals and sticking to them to the finish. It gives people a real sense of accomplishment and achievement. An amateur "contemplates beige" for hours with a customer. They are not decision makers. All doors stay open too long!

Time is really all **we've** got. How we use it makes the difference!

Planning

Definition of Planning:
Someone once said "The purpose of planning is not to show how precisely we can predict the future, but rather uncover the things we must do today in order to have a future."

Common pitfalls to deal with:

1. Loss of control due to ineffective budgeting.
2. Loss of control due to unrealistic scheduling.
3. Loss of control by not organizing for effective action.
4. Loss of control over subcontracts/subcontractors.
5. Loss of profit by too-low estimates, incurring unnecessary risks and insufficient preparation for negotiations.
6. Loss of morale and incentive on the part of project personnel, resulting in overruns and delinquent deliveries.
7. Loss of confidence by the customer.
8. Loss of contract.

Questions we should ask before we start a job:

What efforts are critical to the success of the project?

What levels have been assigned to the planning and control staff?

What efforts extend over a significant period of the project?

Which efforts involve significant expenditures?

How will the project be monitored?

How to Get Organized

Time cannot be managed, saved, stored, stopped, or spent. Don't try to manage time or you will simply become frustrated. Use time only as a measuring stick to determine how effective you can become. Can you increase the number of significant accomplishments within the same time frame? Or can you achieve what you are now achieving in a shorter period of time? When you concentrate on something you can control - yourself - you eliminate many of the frustrations. Start by asking yourself:

1. **Do I have a clear set of goals in writing?** Know what you are going to do when. Always ask yourself, "Is what I am working on now leading me any closer to my annual and lifetime goals? Saving time is to no avail if you have nothing meaningful to spend it on.

2. **Am I using you my daily planner properly?**
   Use it to record more than people, appointments and meetings.
   Use it to plan your week in advance.
   Note when you plan to work on a project.
   Block off work times, going through the mail, returning calls.
   Block off family/friend times.
   Recognize that you cannot do everything.

3. **Am I writing important things down?** Don't rely on your memory. Many ideas and opportunities are lost, mistakes made, and communications stifled simply because we rely on our memories.
   Always carry a notepad with you.
   Record phone calls, action resulting from meetings, ideas that pop into your head, assignments given and received, deadline dates, and of course special events: birthdays, conferences, reviews.

4. **Am I developing the "do it now" habit?**
   If it's unpleasant, do it now and get it over with.
   If it's overwhelming, schedule an hour or two in your planner and work on it daily.

5. **Am I a pack rat?**
Buried in paperwork...magazines...junk mail...
Do you have files that get fatter but are seldom used?
Get rid of them.
If you haven't referred to it in a year chances are you won't.
Take time to reorganize your paperwork.

6. **Am I using my desk top as a storage area?** Clear out your in basket daily. Take the time to put away a project once it's finished.

7. **Am I working smarter rather than harder?**
Always search out better ways to do something.
Utilize idle time........waiting room time...........travel time.
Toss out magazines and retain only articles of interest.
Put them in a **read folder** and read during idle times.
Have a **file folder** with you to organize material you wish to save.
Put deadlines on all meetings.
Keep telephone conversations brief.

8. **Am I caught up in the tyranny of the urgent?**
Concentrate on the 20% of activities that produce 80% of the results. Plan as far ahead as possible.
Accept the fact that you won't get everything done that you'd like to get done without sacrificing your health, friends and family. Remember: there is more to life than work.

9. These eight principles are a must for personal organization:

   A. **Set goals and priorities.**
   B. **Plan and schedule.**
   C. **Write things down.**
   D. **Don't procrastinate.**
   E. **Don't be a pack rat.**

F. Store things in an orderly way.
G. Work smarter, not harder.
H. Avoid the tyranny of the urgent.

You can not manufacture anymore time for yourself.......but you can accomplish more in the time you
have.

This is a condensed outline taken from an article written by Harold L.
Taylor which appeared in the ASID Newsletter.

"Must Do" Items

One of the first items of business for the designer who plans to succeed is to develop a priority list of success rules. There are many well - written "success" books on the market. (Refer to the Recommended Reading List page 364-365)

When I opened the doors of my first studio in 1979, I remember reading a great sales book written by a successful insurance salesman. I typed up rules on individual cards and kept them in front of me on my desk for months. Take one area a week and concentrate on it fully. After one full week has been spent concentrating on each area, review continually throughout the following weeks. Soon professional salesmanship will come naturally. Only practice makes a professional...that's it...so practice, practice, practice.

1. **Enthusiasm**...To be enthusiastic, act enthusiastic!

2. Earnestly **tell your "story"** to 4-5 people every-day...every day!

3. **Take a course in public speaking** if you've never had one and do fear public presentations.

4. Take time to **do things in order of their importance**. Set aside a definite time each week for self-organization; properly plan your time.

5. Think in terms of the **other person's interest:**
   A. Find out what the other person really wants and help them get it. (This is often called finding their hot button.)
   B. When you help someone find what they want, they will move "mountains" to get it.

6. **Be sincere...deserve confidence.**
   "If you would win a man to your cause, first convince him that you are his sincere friend".
   Abraham Lincoln

   A. Bring in your "witness"....(former referrals, clientele, or manufacturer's representatives)
   B. Cultivate the habit of making understatements..not overstatements! Never exaggerate!
   C. Look your best...Look like an expert!

7. **Know your business** and keep knowing it!

8. **Appreciation and praise:**
   A. Speak ill of no one...praise your competitors.
   B. Never forget a customer...never let a customer forget you!
   C. "Love" their property...and praise it, probably no one else does much.

9. **SMILE**...an honest deep-down one. It takes more energy to smile, but it gives more energy in return!

10. **Remember names and faces:**
    A. Impression...get a clear impression of faces and names.
    B. Repetition...repeat their name at frequent intervals and concentrate.
    C. Association...associate with a "picture" in your mind...perhaps their business.

11. **Closing the sale...ACTION:**
    A. Save closing points for the" close" attention...interest...desire...close.
    B. Summarize...let the client summarize whenever possible.
    C. Ask questions..."How do you like it?"

D. Welcome objections...
   "Why do you say that?"
   "In addition to that, is there anything else?"
   Find the key issue...the real reason.
E. Get your order form out early.
F. Ask for their signature and get a check with the order.

Franklin's Rules

Another very old set of rules to live by still makes a lot of good sense today. The following comes from Benjamin Franklin and is entitled Franklin's Rules.

1. **Temperance**...Eat not to dullness, drink not to elevation.

   Sound archaic? We have always had a policy of not mixing alcohol with work. If appropriate, save that social drink until after your work is complete.

2. **Silence**...Speak not but what may benefit others or yourself. Avoid trifling conversation.

   Most client's love to talk about their experiences and stories. Yours, however, are of no real interest so be a good listener and keep your mouth shut whenever possible.

   "Samson slew thousands with the jawbone of an ass.
   Everyday thousands of sales are lost the same way."
   Unknown

3. **Order**...Let all your things have their place.
   Let each part of business have its time.

4. **Resolution**...Resolve to perform what you ought.
   Perform without fail what you resolve.

5. **Frugality**...Waste nothing worth something.
   Especially time. "Time is money" and if you are to be financially successful you will use your time to the utmost!

6. **Industry**...Lose no time.
   Be always employed in something useful. Eliminate unnecessary action. Excess conversation is perhaps the biggest time waster.

7. **Sincerity**...Use no hurtful deceit.
Think justly. Learn as much as you can about your client. Care about their needs - really care.

8. **Justice**...Wrong none.
Never, never overcharge or take advantage of a client.

9. **Moderation**...Avoid extremes. That's a good design rule, too.

10. **Cleanliness**...Tolerate no uncleanliness.
Sloppy files, messy closets, tacky vehicles, scruffy shoes, unkept fingernails, etc.

11. **Tranquility**...Be not disturbed at trifles or at incidents common or unavoidable.

Note Murphy's Law: "If anything can go wrong, it will."

It's hard to remain tranquil when dealing with what might seem to be insurmountable problems - take a deep breath (maybe 2 or 3) and try to keep a smile on too! Always have a large mirror near your phone. Look at yourself when talking to a client. Are you tranquil, undisturbed, in control?

Try Not to be a "Stress Carrier"

Much has been written recently about sources of stress and ways in which people can cope with or manage stress. A less mentioned source of stress - the stress "carrier" - seldom receives much attention. A stress carrier is: a person who gives stresses to others yet seldom seems to be affected by those stresses. A cartoon once depicted such an executive by the caption "I don't get ulcers; I give them." Most offices or businesses have at least one.

The stress carrier may feel uncomfortable when things are going too smoothly and may allow a stressful situation to arise just so they can conquer it.

Some stress carriers are unaware of their actions. Others are very thoughtful and conscious about their contributions to the stresses of others.

Stress carriers can play different roles in the design business. You might find that one of your designers is talented and well liked by both clients and co-workers, but problems are constantly cropping up on their jobs. Several examples of this are as follows:

Example :
Can't cope with backorders

The designer panics every time a product is backordered. They reselect rather than wait for the backordered product or accept mixed dye lots of fabrics, wallcovering, carpet, etc. This inevitably leads to greater problems than waiting for the original order. A great deal of time is spent by the designer and office manager dealing with suppliers, workrooms and reassuring the client that their project will be completed properly.

Example:
Poor follow-through

The designer doesn't take proper notes when meeting with client and/or doesn't follow through properly on servicing. Since clients come to us for service, they expect personal attention from their designer as well as the office staff. The designer's job is not over once the order is signed and deposit received, but only after the project is complete and the final bill paid. (Sometimes a problem arises that can be straightened out to everyone's satisfaction without the designer's involvement. If it can't, then the designer has to be involved.)

Example:
Negative attitude

Everything that happens in the designer's life is a crisis. The car is always breaking down, they have constant and varied health problems and there are always problems with home/personal life. They are so negatively self-involved that they can't rise above negative situations. They expect everyone else's sympathy.

Example:
The Prima Donna

The designer has a superiority complex, treating office personnel as inferiors in both ability and knowledge. This designer is usually very curt and demanding with office staff. The designer will expect office personnel to drop whatever they are working on to help them whenever they need any assistance.

The Bottom Line

Are you a Stress Carrier? We all are at sometime or another. Be aware when you are. A good business does not thrive or grow with a staff full of stress carriers! Learn to be a good business person first and an efficient problem solver.

Safety Valves for Relieving Stress

Coping with stress and stress management are leading workshop titles these days. Interior design is not immune to stress either. Often our clients are so full of stress that even before a job begins there is stress. Understanding their stresses is important in dealing with your own. Some of theirs might be:

- A physical move
- Financial change
- Personal changes in life style or companions

I've found the following to be very helpful safety valves in managing some of my own personal stresses.

1. **Talk about it.** Confide in someone. It helps to share the worries and frustrations.

2. **Work it off.** Physical exercise will alleviate stress. Find a physical outlet that you enjoy to take care of the anger, frustration and pressure.

3. **Help someone else.** It's easy to become self involved when things aren't going smoothly. Doing something for someone else removes you from your own situation and helps develop a closer relationship with the person you're helping.

4. **Set priorities.** Have a list of the two or three most important goals for each day and devote your energy to them. Don't worry about tomorrow's priorities before it's necessary.

5. **Refuse to become a "superperson".** Trying to do everything can create a tremendous amount of stress in anyone's life. Admit that you can't do everything perfectly and take pride in the things you do well.

R-E-L-A-X. . . . . . How to Cope with Stress

The following is a"life-chart" study indicating that illness and accidents often occur around the time of major events in a person's life. The more changes an individual undergoes during a given span, the more points he/she is likely to accumulate. Statistics indicate that a person who scores between 150 and 300 points during a particular period runs a 50-50 risk of falling seriously ill within two years. If the score exceeds 300, the likelihood shoots up to 80 percent.

In the interior design business, you are often working with clients who are coping with excess stress. It is important to note these signs and help them in an understanding way to get through these tough periods in their life.

I often will just pull this chart out and show a client the number of stress points they can score just through the process of building, remodeling or redecorating. We laugh about it together and then I end up by complimenting them on how well they are doing.

Stress Point Chart

Life Event (for self or immediate family member)	Value
1. Death of a spouse	100
2. Divorce (in immediate family)	73
3. Marital Separation (in immediate family)	65
4. Death of close family member	63
5. Personal injury or illness	53
6. Marriage	50
7. Marital reconciliation	45
8. Retirement	45
9. Change in health of family member	44
10. Pregnancy	40
11. Gain of new family member	39
12. Business readjustment	39
13. Change in financial state	38
14. Change to a different line of work	36
15. Change in number of arguments with spouse	35
16. Mortgage or loan for a major purpose	31
17. Change in responsibilities at work	29
18. Son or daughter leaving home	29
19. Outstanding personal achievement	28
20. Spouse begins or stops work	26
21. Begin or end of school	26
22. Change in living conditions	25
23. Revision of personal habits	24
24. Change in work hours or conditions	20
25. Change in residence	20
26. Change in schools	20
27. Change in recreation	19
28. Change in church activities	19
29. Change in social activities	18
30. Mortgage or loan for lesser purpose	17
31. Change in sleeping habits	17
32. Change in family get togethers	16

10 Rules to Keep Thinking Positively

I'll be honest, on occasion I really can become depressed. Perhaps it's the "artist" in me. We all know and have read about great artists who have had severe bouts with depression. But other things have gotten me down: sales slumps, poor cash flow, a fight with a spouse, too much stress.

Whatever the reason, business must go on. When asked, "How's business?" the answer in general must always be up - "It's great!" To stay 'up' can be work.

Not too long after I started my business, my husband had a massive heart attack and retired. Without the following positive points, I would not have survived. These "rules of thumb" should help keep you up when life is really upside down!

1. **Keep your mind uncluttered.**
   Practice ridding your mind of all negative and self-defeating thoughts.

2. **Practice mental alertness.**
   Your mind grows with exercise. Keep your mental radar working.

3. **Cultivate your reasoning powers.**

4. **Feed your mind.**
   Read, listen and observe everything you can. Educate yourself continually through reading and attending workshops and seminars.

5. **Cultivate curiosity.**
   Ask questions when you don't understand.

6. **Organize your thoughts.**
   Practice going from what you know to what you don't know.

7. **Be open.**
   Never dismiss an idea as useless.

8. **Practice objectivity.**
   Always be willing to examine an idea from a variety of viewpoints.

9. **Discipline your mind to work for you.**

10. **Cultivate common sense.**

Energizers

I'm always interested in what motivates energetic people. Whether you work by yourself or are surrounded by others, there are days and perhaps even weeks when one can feel a lack of energy. There is nothing earth-shakingly new here. These are friendly old reminders. I often need to check this list when I'm feeling a little down or overstressed.

1. Be honest with yourself.
2. Take a course.
3. Go to the library.
4. Think positively and SMILE A LOT.
5. Learn to accept what you cannot change.
6. Don't be afraid of failure.
7. Get friendly with leisure.
8. Reward yourself.
9. Learn to love yourself.
10. Work off your anger.
11. Practice self-expression.
12. Get regular vigorous exercise.
13. Dress the way that feels right to you.
14. Seek out good friends.
15. Contact new people.
16. Do something for others.
17. Allot time for daily meditation.
18. Learn to play again.
19. Laugh.
20. Don't try to be perfect.
21. Spend time in a new environment.
22. Take one thing at a time.
23. Develop a hobby.
24. Set up desirable futures.
25. Learn to vary your pace.
26. Plan for maximum comfort.
27. Learn to identify your own need in a relationship.
28. Learn to ask for what you need.
29. Learn to insist.
30. Learn to deal with the answer "no".
31. Learn to identify your limits and boundaries.
32. Learn the limitations of reality.

Others vs. Winners

Others lack the quiet inner strength and motivation that come from a sense of purpose. They suffer from:

> TGIF blues...(Thank God it's Friday)
> Consequences of being late or absent
> Emotional fatigue
> Emptiness of underachieving
> Boredom
> Anxiety
> Depression

Winners make a strong irrevocable commitment to give:

> ALL THAT YOU HAVE ,
> AND ALL THAT YOU ARE ,
> TO ACHIEVE YOUR GOALS!

"I am convinced that my life belongs to the whole community and as long as I live, it is a privilege to do for it whatever I can, for the harder I work the more I live. I rejoice in life for its own sake. Life is no brief candle for me. It is a sort of splendid torch which I got hold of for a moment, and I want to make it burn as brightly as I possibly can before turning it over to future generations."

George Bernard Shaw

What an attitude...what perseverance...what commitment.
An attitude like that can only spell...SUCCESS!

Only when you are totally committed to an overriding purpose will you put forth the effort required to overcome discouragement, misunderstandings and defeat. Consider the bumpy career of one of our great statesmen.

Who:

lost his job in 1832?
was defeated for the legislature in 1832
failed in business in 1833
was elected to the legislature in 1834
lost his sweetheart to death in 1835
had a nervous breakdown in 1836
was defeated for Speaker of the House in 1838
was defeated in bid for Congress in 1843
was elected to Congress in 1846
lost a nomination bid for Congress in 1848
was rejected as a Land Officer in 1849
was defeated for the Senate in 1854
lost the nomination for the Vice-Presidency of the
    USA in 1856
was again defeated for the Senate in 1858
was elected President of the USA in 1860

Answer:
Abraham Lincoln

Quotes to Ponder

As a collector of quotes I thought this would be a good section to share some which have been meaningful to me throughout my business career.

SUCCESS

"Success...the skill of getting up again. . . .a measure of where you are in light of where you began."

Donna Eull Schultz

"To succeed you must be ready to fail. It is only when you realize non-successes are a natural, inevitable part of the process and relax about it, that you will increase your success."

Angelo Donghia

"Nothing left loose ever does anything creative. No horse gets anywhere until he is harnessed. No steam or gas ever drives anything until it is confined. No Niagara is ever turned into light and power until it is funneled. No life ever grows until it is focused, dedicated, disciplined."

Harry Emerson Fosdick

"If you can conceive an idea, you can believe in the idea and then - and then only - You can achieve the idea! You have control over your life when you believe you have control."

Oprah Winfrey

WORK

Work..."Act like a woman. Think like a man. Work like a dog!"

"If people knew how hard I worked to get my mastery, it wouldn't seem so wonderful at all."

Michelangelo

GROWTH

"Growth is not a vertical ascent: I find I take two steps back to take three forward."

Donna Eull Schultz

"I find the greatest thing in this world is not so much where we stand as in what direction we are moving."

Oliver Wendell Holmes

HUMOR

"Humor is POWER!
Laugh at what you can't change.
Otherwise turn negatives into positives!
1. Associate with humorous people.
2. Look for humor in everyday situations.
3. Make your own humor.
4. Look for humor in unpleasant situations."

Jeanne Robertson

EMPLOYEE RELATIONS

"I have yet to find the man, however exalted his station, who did not do better work and put forth greater effort under a spirit of approval than under a spirit of criticism."

Charles Schwab

PROBLEM SOLVING

"Anger is the result of running out of options!"

Peter McLaughlin

TIME MANAGEMENT

"Nothing should be prized more highly than the value of each day."

Goethe

LIFE

"Life is like a grapefruit. First you have to get through the skin, then you have to get used to the taste. Just when your are beginning to enjoy it, it squirts you in the eye!"

BUSINESS

"Having your own business is a grapefruit! Be prepared for regular squirts in the eye!"

"Dig your well before you are thirsty. Do your homework. Know everything you can about your customer. You have to be liked by your customer first."

Harvey McKay

"Not promoting yourself- your services is like a man winking at a pretty lady in a dark room. . . . . He knows what he's doing, why and what he has to offer, however, no one else does."

". . . in today's economy mere creativity is not enough - our clients get creativity with results."

8 Ways to Keep Your Customers Happy

A survey of over 100 top salesmen showed these ways to get and keep new customers:

1. Keep up with your work and follow through when you say you'll do something.

2. Always say "thank you " when you get an order.

3. Sell your products based on customer need, satisfaction and value, not on low price alone.

4. Let your customer know about unavoidable delays and try to obtain an adequate substitute if possible.

5. Learn as much as you can about the customer so that you can talk to him intelligently about his needs.

6. Be a good listener first.

7. Find out who the important decision makers are and take your story to them .

8. Don't knock your competition but be able to compare your products and services with them intelligently.

Reprint from **Executips**

Self-Anaylsis

An exercise I once did with my design staff revealed several interesting facts. So often we perceive ourselves differently than others do.

Get together a small group (4-6 people), who know each other fairly well. (They can be business or social colleagues.) Each person should have as many pieces of paper (all identical shapes and sizes) as there are people in the group. (Example: Five in the group, each person has five sheets of paper in front of them.)

Everyone is then asked to list the five most honest and descriptive adjectives for each of the people in the group. Overall these five adjectives really describe each person effectively. It says how you view the person as a total being. You in turn list the five adjectives you wish would describe you as a total person. They are the words you have personally chosen to indicate how you wish to be perceived by others.

Depending on the closeness of the group, you might want to protect your identity by using identical writing tools and give yourself a large enough area to write, to protect your privacy. When enough time has been allotted, have a little bag or basket with each players name identified. When all are in the bag, each can be passed to it's rightful owner.

The honest results will be most interesting. The words may be more or less than you hoped for. Either way you should get a fairly clear message of how you are perceived by others. The self analysis might give you some insight and direction for subtle or direct changes necessary to enhance your business image. Hopefully, the activity, will be a positive learning experience.

Variations can be more specific such as:

- List five adjectives that describe what each person looks like.

- List five adjectives that describe one's business skills.
- List five adjectives that describe one's attitude.

This activity can be handled in many ways. The closeness of the group really is the key. When a group is not close, however, you might get even more effective results. Follow-up discussion is not at all necessary. More important is the group's preliminary consent and direction for the results they wish to receive.

Here are some other questions you can ask to analyze yourself:

1. Describe briefly what kind of person you see in the mirror.

2. Why should people do business with you? (What image do your clients/ employers /friends /peers have of you?)

3. Last week I made the following efforts to be successful in my career.

4. Last week I could have been more productive if I would have. . .

5. Are you prepared to meet the "Competition" in your career or industry?

6. If you desire to succeed you must "hurt sufficiently". List some hurts:

7. Do you find yourself "bored and full of complacency"?

8. Analyze recent successes and discover "I CAN". (List as many as possible.)

9. Do you play the game "Confession without Change"? (I'm so sorry...)

10. Write specific, measurable (attainable with stretch) goals for the next 12 months with specific plans and methods to achieve these objectives.

Source:
Jerry Smedberg, **"Live, Love, Laugh and Sale on to Success"**

Saying "Yes"

Those who are busy seem to get requests to become busier...over and over again. When one is efficient, competent, and productive, one is most likely to be offered more and more leadership roles. It is often difficult to prioritize one's life. There are so many different directions we can be pulled...family, spouse, children, work, special interests, personal needs and on and on! When does one say, "yes"? I created the following list of questions to ask myself before I say "yes" so quickly. Perhaps it will be of help to you.

1. **Will it help promote my business/career?**
   Yes   No
2. **Will it be O.K. with my family?**
   Yes   No
3. **Can I afford to do it...both in time and costs I would incur?**
   Yes   No
4. **Will I have fun doing it?**
   Yes   No
5. **Will I get paid to cover any expenses I might incur?**
   Yes   No
6. **Will I feel good about myself for doing it after all is said and done?**
   Yes   No
7. **Does it fit into my long-range planning goals for myself?**
   Yes   No

Scoring:
7/7...Go for it!
6/7...Enjoy!
5/7...Why not?
4/7...It's a thinker,check with others for some
         feedback!
3/7...Why?
2/7...No way!
1/7...You must be crazy to even consider it!

Footnote: This might seem too cut and dried for general decision making but it has really helped me prioritize my life quite simply!

System 2: *Communications*

Communication and Success

I have always been a stickler for good communication. If there is one single area that can make or break a potentially successful businessperson's image, I would say it has to do with communication skills. If you do not realize how you are communicating with others, it is important to get some honest, immediate feedback from people you trust and respect. Do not be afraid to ask for it. Asking for feedback is one thing...learning from it is the most important aspect!

WINNING FIRST IMPRESSIONS

Key 1: **Always Put Your Best Foot Forward**
Face to face impressions are formed within
4-6 minutes
Telephone impressions are formed within
45 seconds
Job interviews decisions are made within
30 seconds
Impressions are formed by:
  55% nonverbal
  38% voice
   7% words

Key 2: **Present a Winning First Impression**
Project confidence... (People buy people)
Focus on others..not yourself
Be enthusiastic and energetic
Dress professionally
Smile (be friendly and personable)
Be a walking logo (be unique)

Key 3: **Treat Every Individual as a Valued Person**
Discover something special about each person
Display sincere interest with voice and behavior
Ask questions...and listen to the answers
Include everyone...(stay focused)
Maintain good eye contact

Support others in doing their best
Express thanks and appreciation often

Key 4: **Begin Building Rapport Immediately**
Match rhythm (pace and lead)
Speak their language.....not yours
Use encouragers....avoid killers
Use name of person
Self-disclosure (be real)
Use rewarding non-verbal cues (appropriate
body distance, smile, an occasional arm pat,
good eye contact, pleasant voice)
Listen 70% of the time
Talk 30% of the time, (avoid interrupting and
anxious listening)

People are most comfortable with people like themselves. Mirroring others means to build rapport by pacing
yourself and matching rhythm with your client. If you are
out of sync, you are probably also out a sale!

Malandro Communications, Inc. 1985.

Fee Communication

It is often difficult to discuss fees with a client, especially over the phone or in a group situation that catches you off guard. Take the time to practice and role play your fee communication skills several times with a friend or colleague. Listening to yourself on tape will also provide great insight.

There are several ways interior designers charge for their services.

> • Flat fee
> • Flat fee plus percentage of costs
> • Hourly and per diem fees
> • Cost plus percentage markup
> • Retail
> • Percentage off retail
> • By square foot
> • Combination

I recommend reading A Guide to Business Principles and Practices for Interior Designers by Harry Siegel for a thorough coverage of the pros and cons of each method of charging.

After 15 years as a designer, I am still an advocate of selling retail and to quote Harry Siegel, "retail is unquestionably the most remunerative method of compensation for a designer."

I like to keep things simple for my residential clients so I basically give them two options:

Questions: "How do you work?"
Answer: "Basically one of two ways:

1. **Hourly fee for "Consultation-only" work.**
   An hourly rate is charged for services rendered on short term projects where a professional opinion or space planning work needs to be done.

Typical services provided at on-site consultations:
A. Hanging pictures on the wall.
B. Rearranging furniture and suggesting future needs.
C. Making overall color and interior recommendations.
D. Giving some long range planning direction for furniture selections, flooring, wallcovering and window treatments.
E. Making remodeling suggestions with on-site floorplans and space planning."

Consultations services are recommended for people who have either their own buying sources or have the time and great ambition to pursue the most cost effective resources for their needs. They might also be great do-it-yourselfers.

This method of compensation protects me from clients who are users of 1-800 number shopping resources. When qualifying your client, an important step is to note how they are accustomed to shopping. An hourly fee protects you from being taken advantage of. It is your job as a professional to know your client's shopping habits. You will not change them unless you PPP - preplan to prevent problems!

2. **Retail/Retainer**
   This is best for the client who intends to make purchases through our company. Approximately 10 % of the projected budget is requested as a retainer which is credited after purchases are made. A design fee is usually not charged when purchases are made at a retail level.

   When a client questions "retail" with such concerns as:

   Question: "How do your prices compare to other stores?"

Answer: "Our prices are comparable to better furniture stores, however:
- We have a much wider variety of
sources because we aren't tied to
certain lines carried on the floor.
- Because of our variety of sources, we
have a wider price range to offer.
- We enjoy doing the finishing touches
that large stores don't get involved in
such as several home visits, complete
accessorizing services and art selection
and framing."

Other questions arise such as:
Question: "Do you discount?"
Answer: "Everyday is a discount day for you when
you consider all the extra services and professional design expertise you receive
at no extra charge!"

Question: "What if I find a sofa cheaper somewhere
else?"
Answer: "You can either pay me for my time and purchase it elsewhere or make your purchase
through our studio. I'll be glad to tally up
the hours rendered so you can compare
costs." (Remember these hourly cost should
be kept at all times just for such occasions -
Note time card attached.)

Letter of Agreement - Residential

The following letter of agreement is a tool to qualify your clients. I use it with approximately 90% of my clients. I have revised it several times over the last six years. It has proven simple and easy to use.

DESIGN SERVICES: The designer will provide the following work for the client:

_____

_____

DESIGN AREAS:_____

Preliminary Schedule:

___Planning/Schematic Design   _____

___Design Development   _____

___Procurement/Administration/Intstallation   _____

A. **Retainer** - an estimated budget for the above services and/or materials purchased is $_____. Costs are subject to change upon decisions made by the client. Client shall pay in advance a retainer of $_____, which is estimated to be 10% of the projected initial budget. If this contract is terminated and actual design time(hourly fee) rendered is less than the retainer, the difference will be refunded.

B. **Consultations/Schematic Design Development Services Only:**
Clients using design services only, (procurement/installations done by client) will be billed at the hourly rate of $____. Billing will be after each appointment. Payment is due within 10 days or prior to the next appointment.

C. **Additional Items:**
Certain items may be subject to additional charges:
___Design related installations/accessorizing/shopping (flat fee)
___Overtime/Rush Work (Less than 1 week)
___Supervisory/Scheduling/Receipt of merchandise/services for third party work hired by client
___Other:_____

WARRANTIES AND WORKMANSHIP
We will provide:
1. Professional coordination of fabrics and furnishings and concern for your needs first.
2. Prompt, professional follow-up if problems do arise.
3. Recommended resources that maintain the highest standards of workmanship.

We are not responsible for:
1. Work by third parties not engaged by us.
2. Warranties not provided by our manufacturers and resources.

CLIENT   YOUR COMPANY'S NAME

_____by_____Date_____

I can discuss our letter of agreement easily over the phone. It can be sent through the mail for a client to review. In some cases a client might wish to add their own addendum.

Example:

This letter amends your Letter of Agreement for Design Services dated 9-26-89.

It is our understanding that the $500 retainer will be applied as a down payment for any products we order from or through your company. Specifics are as follows:

1. We intend to spend approximately $5,000 on products.

2. The retainer will cover 10% of our expenditure. For example, if we spend $3,000, $300 will be applied to the purchase, and the other $200 will be your fee for design services. Similarly, if we spend more than $4,500, the entire $500 will be applied to the purchase.

Please acknowledge this letter by signing below. Thank you.

Sincerely.

Listening and Communicating

To be a good communicator one must become a good listener. When working with clients it is most important to listen to what they are telling you, both verbally and non-verbally. Questionnaires are good to use on first appointments to gather pertinent information. (Note New Client Profile page 159 to be used on your first appointment with a client.) These can be filled out later after you've left a client's home. (Be subtle if completing on-site). The following are some benefits from active listening:

Benefits of Active Listening

1. When you actively listen...you learn!
   "Every man I meet is in some way my superior and in that, I can learn from him."
   Emerson

2. When you actively listen, you express interest in the person! You show that you value the person...they matter...when you are actively listening.

3. When you actively listen, you gain insight as to how the person perceives his or her needs, desires and motivations.

4. When you actively listen, you give people an opportunity to let down their guard so they can hear what you have to say.

5. When you actively listen, the other person is involved in the communication process.

6. When you actively listen, you can clarify misconceptions.

Developing Your Listening Skills

Good listening skills can be developed. Here are some guidelines to quality listening habits:

1. **Give your undivided attention.** It shows the "I care" attitude.

2. **Wait your turn.** Don't prepare what you are going to say. If you are doing this, your mind is busy and you're not listening.

3. **Don't interrupt.** Wait until the other party has completed their statement.

4. **Show a friendly smile while listening.** Even if you disagree, this will draw more information from the speaker.

5. **Position yourself** so that everyone necessary is included in the conversation.

6. **Continually question your client** to get a better understanding of what they are saying and what their expectations are.

Don'ts:

Don't fold your arms.
Don't put your hands in your pockets.
Don't fidget with anything in your hands.
Don't express too much non-verbal agreement. You will seem insincere.
Don't be turned off by improper speech patterns or poor English.

Do's:

Do have your hands at your side and palms forward. Lean forward slightly.
Do nod occasionally if you feel you understand what you are being told.

Do watch the speaker's body language.
This will let you know if they are reinforcing their statement and give you additional understanding of what is being said.

Do repeat statements made by the speaker when discussing the conversation to let them know that you heard and understood their statements. This is called paraphrasing.

Do listen carefully to voice inflection. A client may say "no" in many different ways, indicating that a "no" could be very firm or very tentative.

Do maintain direct eye contact.

Well-developed listening skills will yield quicker closes because you will be able to develop your sales presentation directly toward the target of perceived needs, wants and desires of the client. The art of listening and communicating is a science unto itself.

Three Great Barriers To Active Listening

Listening is an art. We so often think the great communicators are the talkers. Wrong - often it is the listeners that people feel the closest to. Think about it. There are hundreds of books out now on communications alone and specifically listening. I strongly suggest taking a course on listening skills and how it relates to good sales communications.

1. **Preconceived Notions.......biases, prejudices, opinions**

   How many times have you prejudged someone? I have many times. The worst part is that I've been wrong! If there's anything I've learned over the years it's that people often give impressions which they really aren't aware of. They're often intent in something and do not realize how they're perceived. Never assume anything. Take the time to really get to know someone. Don't judge a book or a body by it's "cover".

2. **Haste..................lack of time, lack of interest!**

   Haste is one of my main problems. I'm always in a hurry.That can be good and that can be bad. If people feel my haste, it can work against me. I appear to have more important things to do. A good rule of thumb is to assume the pace of the person you are talking with. Take time to appreciate and enjoy your clients. They in turn will appreciate you.

3. **"Agenda Anxiety". . . .what we have to say is more vital!**

   This can be similar to haste. The difference is that our mind is really not on the subject at hand. We are down the road and want to get moving. This shows a lack of sincerity, courtesy and interest to the person we are talking with. It will be noticeable. Be aware of it! Keep your mind focused on what your client is telling you. If they didn't think it was important, chances are they wouldn't be saying it!

"People Skills" Suggestions

Always remember that clients who use interior design services expect to be treated better than customers of McDonald's! McDonald's treats its customers very well so what does that say to you? The following are "people skills" that will help you build and keep your clientele.

1. Learn to be appreciative of people's time.
2. Be prompt.
3. Be willing to serve and help.
4. Offer to help carry their samples or purchases to their car.
5. Learn to say "I'm sorry" when you should.
6. Compliment them when you can.
7. Show interest and enthusiasm in their joys.
8. Show compassion and understanding for their losses.
9. Pay attention to their kids and pets.
10. Become a "temporary" member of their family.
11. Offer to drop things off at their home if it is something you should do in order to sell.
12. Help facilitate the sale in any way possible.

Message Taking

1. Always make sure you are getting the name correctly spelled.

2. Make sure you write down the phone number and company the caller represents. It saves time for someone else having to look it up.

3. Ask what would be the most convenient times to call them. Busy people are seldom in one place for very long. Often we play "telephone tag" with each other. To prevent this, leave suggested times when you know you will be in and reachable.

4. Ask to see if someone else could perhaps help. This gets the client talking and you can get a feeling for the nature of their call.

Ways to Control the Phone

1. Have a "no calls now" time, say "She's with a client now" or "She's in a meeting now".
2. Return calls at a certain time only.
3. Only make calls on your daily list.
4. Make phone appointments.

Call Record

```
Date:                    Time:

Name:

Client_____Potential Client____Rep____Other_____

Phone #:
Best times to return call:
Nature of call:



Follow-up action needed/promised:



Follow-up action completed:_____by whom:_____




Misc:



File in folder_____Throw note_____by whom_____

```

Answering Machine Messages

People who are calling for your company are calling for business or service. They do not need a creatively "cute" message. Be straight and to the point. The following information should be clearly stated and the machine should be easy to listen to.

Example:

"Thank you for calling (your company) a full service design studio. Our regular hours are Monday-Friday from 9-5. Other times are available by appointment. Please wait for the tone, leave your name and number and we'll be sure to get back to you. Thank you for calling."

Note: For good answering machine messages:
1. State **who** they have reached. Always use the word "Interiors" when using the name!
2. State **what** you are...a full service design studio.
3. State when you're usually open.
   Monday through Friday 9-5
4. Stating **where** you're located...might be included although anyone using the phone book should have access to that information. Long distance calls might need this information, however.

Your message should be short and concise. Speak with an enthusiastic, energetic voice. Call yourself a few times and see how good it sounds.

Staff Communications

1. **The entire staff needs to assist in good phone and client message taking.** A message center should be provided. The designer must return all calls on a daily basis. A 24-hour phone call return is recommended unless the Office Manager can notify the client that this will not be possible.

2. **Phone and "drop in" client communications:**
   A. Excellent communication skills with the client and prompt follow through is expected.
   B. Designers should exhibit good communication skills with all subcontractors involved on a job. When involved with new subcontractors all efforts should be made to develop exceptionally good relationships.

3. **Names and phone numbers** of all appointments should be on the designer's desk calendars with the notations as to whether the appointment is in or out of the studio. This calendar should be on the desk at all times with at least one week's appointments/day plans scheduled.
   Calendars should be filled out as follows:

Monday:	A.M. Staff Time
	P.M. Client Presentations
Tuesday:	Client Presentations
Wednesday:	Long Range Planning/ Promotional
Thursday:	Client Presentations
Friday:	Prep Time/ Catch up/Problem Solving

4. **All appointments are expected to be kept promptly.** I suggest that if you are to be more than five minutes late, a call should be made to the client. Professional courtesy is most important. Cancellations or rescheduling is expected to be done at the client's preference. Cancellations should be ideally made 24 hours ahead of appointment time.

5. All personnel **must** begin each day by checking their box for notes and items that need attention. Empty your box daily, processing information according to the numbering priority system below:

#1- within 24 hours
#2- by the end of the week/2-3 days. Discuss that day.
#3- By the end of the month

6. Any new suppliers/sources/workrooms selected by a designer for use **must be approved** and "walked through" by the owner before proceeding with the order/contract. Also have a new source sign a subcontractor form.

7. Correspondence of any kind on business letterhead **must be approved and proofread** before mailing. Common courtesy suggests this be done 24-48 hours ahead, not just before mailing. All contracts and proposals must be approved and proofread.

8. All designers are required to be prepared for a client **24 hours ahead** of a scheduled appointment.

9. When out of the office, all designers must call in at least once a day for messages and twice is even better - appropriate times are in the middle of the day and the end of the day.

10. **Remember VIP clients** with cards and flowers when appropriate. Flowers and plants must be approved by the owner.

11. All clients $3,000 and above should have presentations **pre-approved** at Monday Staff Meetings before presenting to a client. This is for the designer's protection.

Handling a Walk- In Client

Any walk-in client, friend or sales representative could be a potential sale or a potential promoter of your business. It is important to take every opportunity you have to promote your business and "tell your story".

If you have a retail-like space the following points should be considered when and if the situation allows.

1. Introduce yourself with your polished one-minute commercial.
2. Tell them what services you offer. Make them feel comfortable about design services. Review the myths around interior design.
3. Help them understand that you are not expensive... you work within budgets. Show them your design portfolio.
4. Educate them to the fact that designers are trained facilitators who assist them with their decision making...much like a travel agent! It doesn't necessarily cost them more.
5. Walk through your design space. Let them see that you sell more than just "wallcovering". Stress all the products you work with.
6. Get them to fill out a lead card to be on your mailing list, if you have one.
7. Discuss their needs. Ask open-ended questions. Set up an appointment if there is a need and a workable budget.
8. Discuss how you work and how you charge.
9. Invite them to any special upcoming events, if applicable.

When Manufacturer's Representatives Drop In

Be Professional!

1. If your schedule is tight, and a salesperson drops in without an appointment, ask that they leave their card, with a brief description of their line, and you will call back later to set up an appointment.

2. If possible, schedule one day a week with a one hour time frame especially reserved for manufacturer's reps. Schedule one half hour per rep, let them know of your procedure and the amount of time alloted for their presentation. This system allows you to pre-screen those manufacturers you are really interested in hearing from. It also encourages professionalism.

3. Gather pertinent information and sampling data. Sales representatives can offer a wealth of information. Learn the appropriate terminology. If you feel weak in a particular area, take time out to set up an appointment with the appropriate sales rep.

4. Analyze their salesmanship - their professionalism, their strengths and their weaknesses. Are they a professional or an amateur? Do they really solve problems for you? Are they really knowledgeable? Do they know how to listen?

5. Don't trade stories with them.

How to Succeed as a Sales Representative

Many of us have been guilty, at one time or another, of treating sales representatives, commonly referred to as reps, as second-class citizens. I feel that anyone who comes into a place of business, be it to sell or buy something, deserves to be treated in a pleasant manner. Respect, however, is something we earn!

The following suggestions are useful for anyone in sales. Follow them when calling on new accounts as well as when you are talking to established accounts.

1. **Call first to make an appointment.** State your true purpose. Clarify how long the appointment will take. If it is not possible to call first, stop by and leave your card with a written message asking the client to call you to make an appointment.

2. **Once the appointment is made, be on time.** If you are delayed, call and let the client know. Then set a new time to meet. Reiterate the length of your appointment and stick to it. Don't linger to chat.

3. **When making your presentation, make sure it is just that** - a well-executed, polished, and professional presentation explaining the products or services you are selling. Make sure you are as knowledgeable as you should be. Do your homework on the company before the appointment! Take everything you need with you. Be meticulously organized.

4. **Ask how you may be of service.** Be a good listener. Take notes and follow through promptly in writing or with a call.

5. **Be a creative problem solver.** Too many people in sales fail grossly when it comes to solving problems. Great sales representatives solve problems daily.

6. **Observe a successful sales representative at work.** What does he or she do that makes people buy?
Here are some unproductive sales habits that bother me. Avoid them at all costs.

A. **Aloofness**. . . the tendency to make one feel as if it is a big favor for the sales rep to show me their wonderful product line.

B. **Merchant flaunting**. . . the tendency to flaunt major accounts by telling what the big boys are buying. This habit either makes me want to:
   1) Order something totally different from another company.
   2) Order nothing.
   3) Distrust the sales rep because I feel he or she is just trying to make a sale rather than carefully guiding me into a good decision.

C. **Problem avoidance**. . . the habit of saying something like, "We've never had anyone complain about that before" or "That's never ever happened before." This makes me feel like I have no right to discuss the problem. Positive problem solving techniques such as asking key questions and providing possible solutions with understanding are far more appropriate. Every product has potential problems, so why pretend they don't exist. A good sales representative solves problems quickly and stands tall behind their merchandise or services.

These common mistakes are made by *un*professionals. Take a close look at yourself and see if you fit into any of these categories. All of our potential customers are making decisions on whether or not to buy from us based on how professional we are!

Written Communication

Written communication is equally as important as verbal communication. The spoken word can be forgotten but the written word is there in black and white and can not be called back or forgotten once a letter or written communique has been sent. Be careful!

Nothing should go out in the mail until it has been proofread!
Good memos, letters, and notes don't just happen...they're planned. Before you write the first word:

1. Decide what you want to say. Make it concise.

2. List all the points you want to cover.

3. Organize your points.

4. Make a rough draft. Note sample letters throughout this book.
   A. Potential client letter
   B. General thank you letter
   C. Thank you after problem letter
   D. Consultation end letter
   E. Retainer end letter
   F. Reference letter

5. Write letters with the reader in mind:
   A. Personalize it.
   B. Be positive.
   C. Be pleasant.
   D. Use "safe" language. . . avoid something that you might laugh at later, i.e., tongue-in-cheek expressions or jargon that can be misconstrued.
   E. Be concise.
   F. Don't play games.
   G. Make it interesting.

6. Letters should be appealing and easy to read. Make everything about your correspondence jump out at the reader and say...READ ME!

A. Use the attractive business letterhead or cards.
B. Keep it clean.
C. Spell correctly...(remember the proofreading rule!) If you are alone, take more time to proofread and read your work out loud. Use the dictionary.
D. Make it easy to read.
E. Dress it up...If it's important...underline. Layout is very important!
F. Use reader's aids...numerals, lists, outlining.
G. Don't be pretentious.

Potential Client/Residential Letter

Dear Potential Client:

Thank you for calling us about your design needs. Enclosed is a brochure and information regarding our services. Please do not hesitate to call if you have any questions concerning our services. We look forward to hearing from you in the near future.

Sincerely,

MEMOS:

1. It is a good idea to hand write this note on your stationery.
2. Don't forget to mark your calendar and follow-up on this letter in a week.

General Thank-You Letter

Dear Client:

It has been a pleasure working with you on your home. We hope you are pleased with the end results. I see many special 'touches of class' throughout.

Any referrals to other friends would, of course, be greatly appreciated. A few cards are enclosed for this purpose. We would appreciate your completing and returning the enclosed client review form* if you have any comments to share. Remember us for business design also. Enclosed is our reference list for that area.

Sincerely,

*Client Review Form is on page 169.

After Problem to Client - Sample Letter

Dear Client:

I wanted to thank you again for your patience concerning your (problem). I am very pleased that the end result was even better than the first. I most certainly appreciate good clients, such as yourselves, and I cannot thank you enough for your patience throughout this process.

I look forward to seeing you again soon.

Sincerely,

Follow-Up Letter to Supplier on Problem

Dear Supplier:

This is a twofold letter. First of all, thank you for "saving" our ABC Co. account by making a swift delivery of new goods to the site - 44 yards of J.P. Stevens Coloresque/ Old Straw on our PO # 1288-ABC. We are most appreciative of this special attention. That's the way we run our firm and it's nice to do business with efficient companies.

Secondly, we did incur extra moving/labor costs. We were able to adjust this amount down in cost with our installer due to the circumstances. Enclosed is a copy of a statement for $40.00. We expect to deduct this amount from our carpet distributors invoice because:

1. The initial carpet problem was not due to our errors or omissions.
2. The problem was not due to our installer's errors or omissions.

Thank you for your cooperation on this matter.

Sincerely,

Regarding an Invoice - Sample Letter

Dear Supplier,

In January I visited your showroom in Dallas and ordered two mushroom seats from Monnie. We received an invoice #DAL06659 and we paid $230.00 + $16.00 freight and packing for a total of $246.00. In April we received another letter informing us that the seats were out of stock and we would have to wait for a new shipment. In June we received another letter stating that we could receive the mushroom seats faster if they were shipped from Carmel, California, although the freight might be a little more than if they were shipped from Dallas.

On July 24th the mushroom seats arrived along with a freight bill of $203.93. We should have been better informed at the showroom of the total freight costs and feel you have an obligation to cover these expenses. We certainly are not used to having the freight costs be as much as the items purchased.

Please reply.

Sincerely,

Consultation End - Sample Letter

Dear Client:

I enjoyed spending time with you during our consultation, and hope I gave you many good ideas. If you need any further assistance please do not hesitate to call. Your house is great!

I have enclosed a couple of my business cards. We have built our business from referrals from satisfied clients. We would appreciate your passing these on to friends with design needs.

Thank you again for the opportunity to help.

Sincerely,

System 3: *Getting Started*

Business Imaging

Lately the term "imaging" or being "visionary" has become quite popular. I had lunch with a banker friend recently who chuckled as he talked about all the potential new business owners who come into his office asking for loans because they have a "vision" of a potentially successful business. I replied, "Don't knock it - having a vision is a very important place to start!" But it's only a beginning we both agreed.

For at least five years before I opened and bought the property for our business, I visioned a house on a busy street as the perfect studio site. I visioned the inside - how I could space plan it - a kitchen with great kitchen ideas and accessories - a living room with a room arrangement, accessories and appropriate catalogs. By visioning the site so strongly, I was ready to make the commitment when the opportunity presented itself.

We bought a run down house on a five-acre parcel for our business site. The property was zoned agriculture on a soon to become major intersection/highway. I started by working out of the basement/lower level. (Never say basement. Always say Lower Level.) When asked, "Do you work out of you home?" I learned to smile and say, "No, we live in the upper level of our studio!" (Always say: "we/our". Never say "I/me".) Remember to the world, bigger is better and there are a lot of people working with you and for you "behind the scenes".

Imaging or visioning is a first step in the preplanning process. It is where goal setting begins. Try this exercise for fun. Take the time to actually write out your thoughts - a very important part of goal setting.

Close your eyes for about five minutes. Put your feet up. Close out all other thoughts and commitments. Then:

1. **Visualize** how you'd like to be described as a professional five years from now:

> **Examples:**
> One of the top 10 designers in your area
> One of the most creative designers in your area
> A successful designer/business person
> One of the best drapery workrooms

2. **Imagine** your working environment - visualize the ideal setting - location:
   Examples:
   A small studio
   A studio in a retail setting
   An office-like environment
   An office in a commercial area
   With a major growing company
   With an innovative aggressive franchise

How you will be viewed and where you will be working are two preliminary steps in goal setting. You might talk with several other people to get some feedback on the path you are setting up for yourself.

Your **USP (Unique Selling Position)** should also be determined and imagined. How will you be unique from your competitors? This is how you visualize yourself set apart from your competition. Reality might be something quite different but when it comes to marketing - the name of the game is to set yourself up as something unique - special - the best available option!

It is interesting to look at another product for analogies. Consider soft drinks for example. There are dozens of soft drinks. Each one, however, tries to set themselves a part from the others. Their marketing ads and jingles keep reminding us how unique their taste is.

"For me, success is a measure of where I am in light of where I began and where I hope to be."

Donna Eull Schultz

Site Guidelines

The majority of independent designers work out of their homes. I did that for five years before expanding. There are pro's and con's for everything. Consider the following if you are looking at new business directions.

1. The home-like atmosphere is friendly, warm, and inviting...all of which help to break the traditional image of interior designers being "uppity".

2. A home-like setting eliminates everyday "walk-in" clientele which can take up a lot of your time.

3. Serious clients will call first and check on your hours and your terms.

4. A house set up can be great for adjacent living quarter facilities. This must be kept totally separate, however. If living quarters are planned for, the studio might be on one level with a separate entrance. Be sure local zoning regulations are acceptable for this set-up. Rezoning (if possible) is very costly, as well as time-consuming.

   a. Advantages: All of the above plus tax advantages.
   Flexible hour arrangements.
   Being close to one's work.
   No driving hassles.

   b. Disadvantages: Living too close to one's work.
   Less walk-in opportunities.
   Judged by some as being less professional.

Other alternatives:
1. Strip mall studios

   a. Advantages: Walk-in traffic and a chance to be very visible and very professional looking.

   b. Disadvantages: Flexible hours might not be available.
   Non-ownership of building.
   No equity build-up in building.

2. Commercial building space
   a. Advantages: Quiet......minimal walk-in trade.
   Flexible hour opportunites.

   b. Disadvantages: No equity build-up.
   Non-ownership of the property.
   Minimal walk-in trade.

There are no magic set of rules for success in site location.   Success is based on what you do with what you have.

Square Footage Recommendations

A small studio/office requires 600-1,000 sq. ft.   A larger studio would require approximately 1,200-2,000 sq. ft.

Leasing Guidelines

The following is a list of suggestions to consider when negotiating a lease.

1. If your business is fairly well established, negotiate a lease for as long a term as possible. Three to five years is ideal. Leasehold improvements are already completed and paid for the first year. Try to negotiate for no increase rental costs for the next five years.

2. Do not get involved in percentage rents. This is when the landlord requests a percentage of your sales as revenues increase. If this is mandatory, choose a sales figure that you know you won't be able to reach the first year (such as 5% over a million in sales).

3. Negotiate for approximately $3 less than the asking rate (square footage rates).

4. Don't get involved with CPI (consumer price index) leasing. This is where the rent is based on the CPI Index and will probably go up. The builder's/owner's costs should be fairly fixed as the building is up and-complete.

5. Get new construction dollars from the landlord. These are often available for leasehold improvements.

6. Request a usage clause. This states what you are going to do with your space such as selling furniture, draperies etc. This protects you if they change their usage plans.

7. Request flexibility in trademark or name. If you have to change your business name for some reason you are protected from being forced out.

8. Request approval for new neighboring tenants. This will protect you from a new tenant whose image or business could be a negative factor for your business.
   Example: • Raquetball Court
   • Belly Dancer Restaurant

Setting Up Your Studio

You will be judged by others on the way your working environment appears. It does say something about your professionalism. Consider the following areas in your planning:

1. **Reception Area**
2. **Planning - Samples - Work Area - Delivery - Storage**
   a. Retail Inventory Space...where stock items such as art, accessories and easily placed furniture and lamps might be displayed.
   b. Client-Presentation Areas...as your studio grows it might be advisable to have at least two conference areas where other staff members can meet and confer with clients or sales people.
   c. Sample Room...for wallcovering, carpet, window treatment books, catalogs, fabric samples.
   d. Storage...for wallcovering, window treatments and other items that come in regularly.
   e. Office Manager's Space...desk for typing, pricing, catalogs, files.
   f. Designer's Work Space...drafting table, supplies.
   g. Layout Space...usually located near sample room.
   h. Computer Workstation.

Manufacturer's reps often refer to designers working out out their homes as "decorinas". Make sure your space can be confidently shown as a "design studio".

Corporate Look

If you are trying to create a corporate identity, some planning should be done to coordinate:
- your business cards
- your stationery
- signage
- advertisements
- logo
- lettering
- corporate colors

I would suggest taking some time to list the top five descriptive adjectives you would like to have used continually to decribe your business. My adjectives have been the following:

1. **Warm and Inviting**...The coffee pot always on. Brochures and newsletters available. An album of work done, awards and credits available and visible.

2. **Professional and "Classy"**...Corporate colors facilitating a classy look. Neatness has a lot to do with a professional look. My corporate colors have been burgundy, cream and gold.

3. **Progressive and Innovative**...New inventory products and art displayed.   Completed floorplans and creative boards showing ideas and projects in progress.

4. **Intriguing**...A pleasant scent, foliage, and good music to enhance our atmosphere.

5. **Energetic and Efficient**...Professional staff piles of collected "messes", providing a classic and comfortable background.

Hours of Business

Hours need to be established right away to get a business-like feeling even if you are a one-person studio and an answering machine. People get tired of speaking to a machine. It is suggested that you experiment the first month with your needs. Try two days in completly and three days out for appointments. Perhaps the next week you'll try three days **in** and two days **out**. Monday is usually a good day to be in, as well as Friday. Monday is a good day for getting things organized for the week and Friday is a good "catch up" day for what you didn't get done or what you need to attend to for the next week. Make sure your hours are stated on the answering machine.

Sampling

The following is a list of samples for starting a studio: Sampling should be budgeted for or it will eat up all of your profits. Salespeople will always be trying to get you to buy more samples. Know your limits and plan your expenses. It will make it a lot easier to say, "no".

1. **Wallcovering Books**: (Approximate Yearly Budget: $_____)

   Select a step above the typical paint store selections. Keep budget in mind. The bulk of your books should be in a price and style range you know you can sell.

   Contemporary Classics
   Traditional Country
   Solid Toned Vinyls
   Miscellaneous Fillers

2. **Fabric Books**: (Approximate Yearly Budget: $____)

   Books are more frequently used than hanger samples. It is not really necessary to go into hanger samples unless you want to show some variety and some favorites that you would like to sell. Key fabrics to hopefully design rooms around would be another approach to hanger sampling. Most books can be acquired at no cost except for specialty lines with companies such as Brunschwig and Fils, Greff, Schumacher, and other high end lines. Note your needs on the following outline before making additional purchases!

   Upholstery Weight Fabrics:
   Casual solids
   Solid velvets
   Corduroys

   Damask/Tapestry
   Large scale
   Small scale

Cotton Prints
    Large scale
    Small scale

    Plaids-Stripes- Geometrics

Window Treatment Fabrics:

    Casements (Heavy)
    Sheer -118" vs 48"-60"
    Semi-sheers
    Cottons....solids
    Cottons..prints

Bedspreads

    Cottons.....solids
    Cottons......prints

Carpet Samples (Approximate Yearly Budget: $_____)

    Berbers
    Cut pile
    Patterned
    Level loop

Note: Private label whenever possible as this protects
    you from being "shopped".

Catalogs: (Approximate Yearly Budget: $_____)

Inventory

Adding saleable inventory can be fun yet costly. I've always bought what I loved therefore knowing I could sell it. Consider the following carefully before making inventory purchases.

1. Can I sell it in 3 months?
2. Can I double the LIC (laid in cost - Don't forget to include the freight) and sell it?
3. Can I mentally place it in a client's home?
4. Can I build a design plan around the piece?

Preparing for a Grand Opening

I had a Grand Opening for my business even though my first studio was in the lower level of my home. It was a very professional way of announcing to everyone I knew that:

- I was in business.
- I needed their help and support.

The following suggestions will be scaled to the budget you set aside for such an event.

A. **Pre-planning Details**

1. Select a date.................It is wise to allow yourself approximately 2 months to get set up properly in your studio. This depends on how much new ordering you have done. The question will be whether or not to wait for the majority of your new stock or to just get up and open! Late afternoons and into the evening seem to be the best times for Open House events. This allows those leaving work to stop by on their way home. Thursdays from 4-7:30 is perhaps the best time for such an event. Saturdays or Wednesdays are probably the best day for an all-day event.

2. **Decide on your advertising approach..............**

    a. Personal letters to all friends and acquaintances.
        1) Start your lead card list for future newsletters and announcements.
        2) Make sure all addresses are current.
        3) Take time to get all the zip codes.
        4) Invite suppliers and workrooms.

    b. Special newspaper ad.
        1) Design and approve two weeks prior to the ad appearing in the paper.
        2) Request proofreading rights.

 c. Special signs and banners at entrance.
  1) Use eye-catching signs, professionally done.
  2) Incorporate colors and logo wherever possible.

 d. Take the time to make personal invitations by phone or in person.

3. Decide on your menu
 a. Serve with a "touch of class"...therefore don't use chips and dips in plastic bags and containers.

 b. For beverages use bottled water, coffee, tea, wine, or champagne. Transfer bulk wine into carafes for serving.

 c. Food served could be a cheese and meat platter, a vegetable platter, hot or cold hors d'oeuvres, petit fours, cookies, or nuts and mints. This all depends on the time of day you are having your Grand Opening .

 d. It is usually well worth the money to use a catering service. Make sure you know what they plan on serving the food in.

4. Floral Arrangements
 a. One special arrangement can be created for the serving area unless the food is prepared so attractively an arrangement would be unnecessary.

 b. Recognize any staff members with corsages and name tags.

B. **One Week Prior to Grand Opening**

   1. Make a list of the week's "things to do" checklist.

   2. Organize your week so that one major task is done each day.

   3. Assign others to help relieve your "load" if possible.

   4. Save your time for things that really count .... such as the overall appearance of your studio.

   5. Double-check on all previous decisions for scheduling.

   6. Make sure your promotional material is out and up:

      a. Newsletters
      b. Brochures/ Cards
      c. Presention Boards showing work in progress or completed

C. **Final Preparation Details...........(one day prior)**

   1. Get everything set up 24 hours ahead if possible.

   2. Prepare staff for hostessing roles. Role-play possible conversations. Make sure everyone has a job to do and knows their specific role.

   3. Arrange seating to accommodate a crowd.

   4. Think about any last-minute exterior signs that need attention.

   5. Make sure lead cards are out and that guests are encouraged to complete them.

D. **Dressing for the Grand Opening**
   1. Dressing in your corporate colors if possible.
   2. It is better to be tailored and professional looking than too party-ish!
   3. Check hose and jewelry.
   4. Take a deep breath and enjoy yourself...........it's your party!
   5. Don't over indulge!

E. **Follow-Up Suggestions**

   1. Write thank you notes to everyone who sent flowers or something special.

   2. Check over the completed lead cards and respond to anyone indicating design interest.

   3. Make a list of all the things you promised to do for someone and make sure you follow up on this.

System 4: *Employees*

Selecting Employees

Selecting employees must be done with job descriptions clearly in mind before seeking candidates. The following is a recommended list of additional staffing needs for a typical studio:

1. **Office Manager**...employee with secretarial, book-keeping, typing, computer and possibly drafting and design related skills. This will become the first additional staffing position and it must be decided if you want this person to fill two different areas: office work and design related work. It can be great training for a designer with a two to four year degree to apprentice at this level and gradually work into sales with two years experience on the inside. Expertise in product knowledge can be gained at this position.

   Suggestions:
   • Start this person 3-4 days a week until you know you have enough work to keep them busy.
   • Hire on a three month trial basis to begin with.
   • Start with a minimal wage and promise them a significant raise after six months if they are good.

2. If you want a full-time **design assistant**, both two and four year program graduates can work out effectively. There are a lot of graduates available so careful interviewing to get the best is highly recommended. Good drafting capabilites, good verbal communication skills, dress, looks, and personality are all of importance. Only time will tell whether they are the person to fill the job at hand. For me, a three month trial period worked out best for all parties. It is suggested that a new graduate, (design assistant) work two years as an assistant before she/he is given any clients. Exceptions can be made once you feel really comfortable or if they bring in their own leads through their own networking.

3. **Designer**...When you reach a point where you and your design assistant cannot take care of all your clients' needs, it is probably a good idea to consider hiring another full time designer. It is strongly suggested that this be postponed as long as possible and serious thought be given to your long range goals at this time. You are apt to be more profitable by having good assistants than more designers. Designers are apt to come and go. Commission payments, draws and designer style can create many additional problems. Experience is worth a lot. A very significant reason for adding another designer would be if you are at a point that you do not wish to have evening or weekend appointments anymore.

4. **Account manager**....for all invoicing, bookeeping and financial work. This might be a part time position to begin with or could be handled by the office manager intially.

Interviewing Techniques and Questions

1. Personal appearance is extemely important in the interior design business. This can be assessed early in the interview.

2. Grammar...listen to see that their speaking habits are acceptable. Get them to talk. "Tell me about your last job." Never ask questions which can be answered with a 'yes' or a 'no'.

3. Why did you leave your last job? What type of a position are you seeking?

4. Would you be uncomfortable in a non-smoking environment? This is very tricky to handle. I recommend that employees do not smoke on the job. Samples absorb smoke which can be offensive to non-smoking clients. Each owner will have to deal with this on an individual basis.

5. Describe the position available and your studio objectives.

6. Ask them what their questions and concerns are about the job?

7. Ask them what their main strengths are and how they can be used in your studio. Why should you consider hiring them over someone else?

8. Ask them to tell you what their weaknesses are and any other personal situations which might be applicable.

9. Salary...Ask them to state their needs but explain that everyone starts out at a "minimal" wage until they prove themselves. This can change rapidly within the first year.

10. Check their references for sure. What does their last employer have to say about them?

Application For Employment

Personal Information

Name

Address

Phone

Referred by

Education
Name and Location of School
High School

College/Vocational School

Years attended*
Year Graduated*
Major

Professional Affiliations

Physical Record

Do you have any physical defects that preclude you from performing any work for which you are being considered?

*The Age Discrimination in Employment Act of 1967 prohibits discrimination on the basis of age with respect to individuals who are at least 40 but less than 70 years of age.

Former Employers (List below last two employers, most recent first.)

Dates	Name/Address/Phone Supervisor's Name	Salary	Position	Reasons for Leaving
1.				
2.				

References (List two people not related to you, whom you have known at least one year.)

Name	Address/Phone	Business	Years Known
1.			
2.			

Emergency Contact Person
Name
Address
Phone

I authorize investigation of all statements obtained in this application. I understand that misrepresentation or omission of facts called for is cause for dismissal. Further, I understand and agree that my employment is for no definite period and may, regardless of the date of payment of my wages and salary, be terminated at any time without previous notice.

Date:
Signature:

Employment Contract

This is a sample of our employment contract. You need to develop one you feel comfortable with.

Agreement dated this _____ day of _____, 19___, by and between (The Company)_____ and_____, (The Employee).

WHEREAS, Company desires Employee to work for Company, and
WHEREAS, Employee desires to work for Company, NOW THEREFORE, the parties mutually agree as follows:

1. Employment and Duties: The Company agrees to employ the Employee and Employee accepts employ-ment as a_____ of the Company and to devote his/her full business time and efforts to the dili-gent and faithful performance of his/her duties, and to abide by all matters covered in the Company's current policy manual. Business time is a _____ hour a week minimum.

2. Term of Employment: Unless sooner terminated for breach of any conditions herein, Employee's employ-ment shall commence with the date of this agreement and shall continue thereafter until terminated by either party on not less than fifteen (15) days written notice to the other.

3. Compensation: Company shall pay employee $_____ per month, payable _____.
Such salary/commission/draw shall be subject to monthly reviews. If after three months a designer's draw is not surpassed by commissions earned or monthly sales goals are not met, the Company will make continued compensation at its discretion.
A deficit draw situation of more than one month's draw will require immediate review of employment compensation. Commissions will be paid only after a sale is paid and complete. It is intended that after

a three month draw period, the designer should be well on their way in terms of monthly sales goals. Monthly sales goal to be averaged after one year's tenure: _____.

4. Confidentiality: Employee will not disclose during or after his/her term of employment any information of the Company that a reasonable individual would deem confidential.

5. Covenant Not to Compete: The Company does not permit any employee to compete with the studio. This includes having outside accounts and relationships with suppliers. Part time positions in design related fields must have owner's approval.

6. Complete Agreement: This agreement constitutes the entire written agreement between both parties, and can be amended only by a writing by both parties.

IN WITNESS WHEREOF, the parties have executed this agreement the day and year first above written.

EMPLOYEE   COMPANY

by:_____ by:_____
Address:
Phone:

Employee Training

1. If your company runs well, but you are currently indispensable, start training people now. Be aware of how your disability might effect your company and your financial well being.
2. Each of your employees should expect to learn something new everyday. As the manager, you should assist your employees in selecting educational books, tapes, or courses, and the company should pay for the material.
3. Salespeople should be in direct contact with the vendors. If one of your vendors wants to take you to lunch to promote a new line of products make sure your sales staff is present to get the product informtion first hand.
4. Hold regular staff meetings - no matter what the size of your company - two people or two thousand people. Each employee should keep track of the things they would like to discuss at the weekly meeting. It's an excellent forum for discussing customer complaints, new product or service ideas. (see Weekly meeting outline on page 106)
5. Consider an on-the-spot cash reward to an employee with a money-saving or money-making idea. We have often awarded special monthly or quarterly bonuses for above average work.

Staff Goal Sheet

In order to progress three months from now - goals have to be made. Writing goals down on paper can be very difficult for most people. Writing them down however, is very important. Seeing them in black and white will help you focus on the tasks at hand.

The next step is to dedicate at least one day a week toward the accomplishment of these goals. Goals can be changed. No one was ever "shot" for changing their goals. Writing goals is step one toward true growth and professionalism.

```
Date:

My goals for the next three months as they relate to my
job are:




I expect to accomplish them by:




Signed:
```

Task/Goal Worksheet

Here is another variation of a goal sheet:

---

1. What are you going to do?

2. Why? What are your objectives?

3. How are you going to do it?

4. Who is going to do it?

5. When (or by when) are you (or "we") going to do it?

6. How much will it cost?

7. What are the expected results?

8. How will we measure the results?

Staff Member:_____

Weekly Sales Report

This is a form that I have used with sales staff. It keeps them organized and assists them in reporting back to the owner. When one is highly motivated, all of this becomes innate and forms are unnecessary.

Week:_____

Client sales
1.
2.
3.
4.
5.
6.
7.
8.
9.
10.

Sales (Leads)
1.
2.
3.
4.
5.

Networking
1.
2.
3.
4.
5.
6.

Self-education
1.
2.
3.

Comments:

Daily Activity Checklist

These are some daily sales motivators to consider:

_____ 1. Be at work no later than 8:30 a.m.
_____ 2. Make a contract appointment.
_____ 3. Sign one contract.
_____ 4. Sell a consultation appointment.
_____ 5. Find a new client.
_____ 6. Get a qualified lead from a former client.
_____ 7. Contact two former clients.
_____ 8. Write a follow-up letter.
_____ 9. Do something positive for your studio.
_____ 10. Read something to help your business.
_____ 11. Go to a networking event.
_____ 12. Develop a new creative idea.
_____ 13. Work more than eight hours.
_____ 14. Solve a design problems.

Weekly Staff Meeting Outline

1. General Staff Business (Memos/Studio Needs)

2. Staff Update Reports (Old Business/New Business)
   A. Customer Service Department
      1) Scheduling

      2) Ordering Needs/Accounts

      3) Problems
         a. Clients
         b. Shipping
         c. PPP (Preplan to Prevent Problems)
            Program Upcoming Concerns

      4) Vendor Communications

   B. Operations
      1) Staff Needs

      2) Studio Needs

   C. Accounting
      1) Past Due/Collections

      2) Invoice Questions

      3) Credit Questions

      4) Sales/Promotions

      5) Price Changes

   D. Public Relations/Networking Opportunities/New
      Leads/Funnel System

   E. General Communications
      Staff sharing events attended for the firm.

Monthly Sales Projections

This sheet is written the last day of each month for the next month. It stays on my desk top daily. It keeps me focused. I always focus on my top accounts. I yellow highlight each client after I have completed my sales goal for the month. Names are added weekly. It's my sales worksheet. Without it, it's easy to lose focus. This will give you an idea of how I fill mine out.

Month: April

Client	Products	Approx. Amt.
Johnson	draperies	$3,000
	wallcovering	
Smith	sectional	$6,000
	coffee table	
Jackson	dining chairs	$6,000
Carboni	artwork	$1,500
Nelson	area rug	$6,500
	3 chairs	
	wallcovering	
Tomkinson	furniture	$10,000
Crockett	accessories	$2,500
	Subtotal:	$35,500

Mid-Month Check-up:
Misc. Add-on's - potentials

Calmut	accessories	$1,500
Pearson	windows	$2,500
Baker,Inc.	consult only	$800
Bracken	tables	$3,000

End of Month Actuals: $34,200

Analysis:
• Keep working on Bracken
• Drop Calmut
• Much more to come with Johnson

Designer Checklist

I never permanently hired a designer on staff until we had worked together for a three month internship period.

I asked them to complete the following form within the first three months. These requests were made for their benefit so that they were comfortable with policies and presentation procedures. A copy was to be completed and on file prior to their three month reviewal.

___1. Read and understand our Operations Manual and/or policies.

___2. Attend three "consultation only" appointments with the owner/senior designer.

___3. Conducted three consultations with the owner/senior designer critiquing.

___4. Attend three "first" appointments where a contract is signed and a retainer collected.

___5. Attend three appointments where a sale/closing is completed.

___6. Be involved in a "whole house" measurement appointment

___7. Complete the additional forms:
_____ Three month goal sheet
_____ Resume/application on file

Date:
Designer's Signature:

Note: Referrals were given by our company when we were confident that the designer was qualified to proceed with our policies and procedures. It is important for the owner/design manager to make sure that a staff designer is qualified in space planning, product specification, color coordination, presentations and communication skills according to your company's standards. In the first three months, I would recommend that all $3,000 orders and above are approved by the owner/design manager before final presentation is made with the client.

Commissions - Hourly Wages

If you have staff designers, chances are a commission on sales is being paid. I found that between 7-10% on a retail sale was average in our metropolitan are. Even if you are an independent designer, it is important to stop, and think once in awhile about what you are actually earning for the hours you put into a job. The following has been helpful to consider remembering that time is money.

A. $660.00 sale
   x   7%
   $46.20 Commission

   $46.20 divided by 4 hours = $11.55 per hour

B. $11.55 per hour
   x   8 hours per day
   $92.40
   x   5 days
   $462.00 per week
   x 4 weeks
   $1848.00 per month.
   x   12 months
   $22,176.00 per year

This is only one example. If the $660 sale only took one hour that would equate to $46.20 per hour.

The purpose of this mental exercise is to be fully aware that "time is money" - our money.

It is my opinion that this is the main reason many designers are unable to support themselves. Too much time is spent making design decisions. Too much time is spent "pondering beige".

Only when you begin to set time limits and produce quality design work within the allotted times, will you begin to make a living as a professional designer.

Commission Sheet

Period:
Designer

PO	Client's Name	Product%	Amt. of Sales	Commission	Paid

33 1/3%	Consultation
	Product Mark-up (ordered directly)
10%	100% +
7%	60-80%
5%	40-50%
	Showroom Product Discount (ordered through show-rooms)
7%	40% +
2%	20-30%

Employee Review Form

	Excellent	Average	Poor
Job Description			
Daily Tasks			
Weekly Tasks			
Monthly Tasks			
Communication Skills			
With Client			
With Staff			
With Sub-contractors			
Organizational Skills			
Attention to Detail			
Time Usage			
Dependability			
Concern for Funnel System			
"Teamsmanship"			
Design Skills			
Creativity Shown			
Versatility			

	Excellent	Average	Poor
Prioritizing Skills			
Budgetary Concerns			
For Client			
For Firm			

Miscellaneous Comments:

Name:

Date:

One Minute Managerial Suggestions

1. When an employee needs correction, try to take the time to do it as soon as possible. Illustrations will be fresh in your mind.

2. Keep your corrections short and to the point. Don't overkill.

3. Speak with an employee individually if you are making corrections.

4. Praise publicly as often as possible.

5. Don't let things build up when there is a staff problem.

6. Do praising at another time if your main intent is to correct.

7. Don't intellectualize. People want to know how you feel. Give it to them straight. For example, "I feel angry because you said you'd checked these figures closely and the total was correct. Your inaccurate report delayed everyone. That really frustrates me."

8. Reaffirm the employee's worth. This is probably the most important point of all. You might say, "Let me tell you one other thing. You're one of our best people. That's why I'm angry about this expense report. I count on you to set an example for others. That's why I am not going to let you get away with this type of careless reporting. You're better than that."

From: **The One Minute Manager** by Kenneth Blanchard and Spencer Johnson

Employee Dismissal

This is not an easy task, but if an employee is more of a "load" or strain than an asset, it has to be done...quickly and without hard feelings. Losing a job is a blow to the ego and a blot on someone's employement record. In this day and age one could be sued or have to pay unemployment compensation if it is not handled carefully. The following are some guidelines to help with this potential situation.

1. It is important to keep written documentation of any disciplinary action taken with an employee.

2. The employer must verify when an employee has not fulfilled his responsibilities.

3. Note guidelines from the Equal Employment Opportunity Commission for your state.

4. First offenses that justify immediate firing are: flagrant insubordination, theft, drunkenness, or embezzlement.

5. Offenses that may not justify immediate firing are: poor performance, disruptive conduct, absenteeism, or tardiness.

6. Three month reviews are strongly suggested and can be of great help in keeping a progressive growth atmosphere.

7. Sometimes it is better to end the relationship at the next pay period. Don't give the "bad apple" a chance to spoil the bunch.

8. If an employee must leave for positive reasons, (maternity leave, a move, etc.) it maybe ideal to let them assist in finding their replacement if there is a need. They could help train a new employee without taking a lot of your time. This, of course, depends on your relationship with the employee and your trust level.

System 5: *Daily Operations*

Business Operating Guidelines

Introduction

The following guidelines come from our companies policy manual. They are included in this section as points to consider when you have a staff of four or more. In our firm two full time administrative people take care of all order placement, customer service, accounts receivable and payable. These positions are referred to as the Office Manager - (Order Placement, Installation, and Customer Service) and Accounts Manager - (Accounts Receivable and Payable).

Potential Clients

1. Lead cards are completed for all new clients. All information should be kept current and dated. (See sample lead card on page 147).

2. Develop marketing skills.
   Networking and Prospecting: An internship of approximately six months with the owner will be required to develop skills in obtaining new clients. **You are responsible for scheduling these opportunities weekly.**

For Remodeling Clients

1. No remodeling job should be done without the involvement of the owner. A minimum of two subcontractors should be recommended to a client when billing does not go through the studio. It is the designer's responsibility to inform the client that the studio is not liable for the workmanship of the subcontractor when not billed through the studio.

2. All remodeling jobs requiring you to act as a general contractor must have a notice of lien rights attached. (See page 231 on Liens)

Processing Orders

1. All quote sheets must be signed and carefully reviewed by the client including the appropriate deposit (30%-50% minimum before order placement.)

2. Quote sheets are to be completed in full by the designer. (See samples) It is the designer's responsibility that all prices are current and billed according to guidelines. Pricing should be approved by the Accounting Manager.

3. Keep all sources to yourself. Give only information needed for accuracy of details on job inclusions. Note: all costs related to the job should be listed on the back side of the yellow sheet.

4. Copies of completed orders are processed as follows:
   White copy - to client
   Yellow copy - client's file/designer use
   Pink copy - to Office Manager/Accounting Manager

5. Time requests for order placement - Within 24 hours of receipt of deposit and signed quote sheet.

Client Folders

All client's folders should be organized in three parts:
Part 1 -   White quote sheets, invoices, account card copies which are to be given to the client at the next appointment should be clipped to the front of the folder.
Part 2 -   All yellow copies of SOLD materials stapled sequentially in order of placement
Part 3 -   Papers clipped and grouped which include notes and floor plans. Client contract should be stapled to the back of the folder.
Note: All samples and cuttings should be stapled to quote sheets or inside of folder.

Invoicing

1. All invoices should be sent within 10 days of completion/installation delivery. That is the responsibility of the designer and Accounting Manager together. Wording of the invoices must be carefully approved by the designer and/or owner. It is strongly suggested that the designer visit the site to approve workmanship, collect final payment and look for continued phases to develop or leads/referrals at this time. Share in the final joy with your client.

2. Payment policies are as follows:
   A. A 50% deposit (30% may be acceptable when needed on orders with costly installation fees and extreme length of delivery) is received on all orders.
   B. Visa/Mastercard financing is available but should be factored into pricing (add 3%). A client should not know about about this "3%" increase! This percentage may vary from state to state.
   C. Any changes due to a customer's situation must be approved by the owner.

3. All designers must submit consultations and bills to the Accounting Manager immediately (within 24 hours) after consultation appointments. They will be invoiced immediately and the designer is instructed to collect for this consultation at the time of the next appointment.This:
   A. Enables the client to keep current and review what they are getting for their money.
   B. Enables you to stay out of trouble if the client is not "happy"/cut your losses ASAP.
   C. Enables you to improve you cash flow.

4. When receiving checks from a client please see that the memo line is completed as to its purpose - retainer or deposit on account. Checks should be forwarded to the Accounting Manager's box.

Problem Solving

All orders incurring problems or complaints on the part of the client/designer must have problem forms on the issue at hand. (See pages 135-139 on Problem Solving) These should be initiated by the designer or the office manager and copies given to the accounting manager for immediate attention on invoices.

Design Staff

1. Commissions/Draw Policy
   A. Designer's are required to keep accurate documentation of monthly sales. (See sample of Commission sheet on page 110)

   B. Commissions will be paid only upon completion of a job and receipt of final payment. All designers are expected to complete their own commission sheets to be turned in at the end of the month. They are encouraged to work with the Accounting Manager on which clients have paid.

   C. Quotation of current prices and bidding or estimating must be done within guidelines if a commission is to be paid. The owner always has the right to adjust commission rates if additional staffing costs occur. The Accounting Manager will assist whenever possible.

   D. A designer (not an outside sales consultant) may receive a six month draw of approximately $500 a month. This is based on doing at least $7500 per month in sales. The initial draw amount can vary depending on the designer's experience and client base and is subject to change at any time. After three months this draw will be reviewed.

E. After six month, average monthly sales will be evaluated as follows:
   1) If sales are below $7500...draw will be removed.
   2) If sales are between $7500 and $12,000 average...cut draw in half.
   3) If sales are between $12,000 and $15,000...the draw will remain the same or increased.

F. Designer's work, attitude and overall professionalism will be carefully evaluated.

G. Designer's may be able to earn additional wages as follows:
   1) General office work
   2) Drafting work...the design manager must negotiate for maximum hours the job should entail. The owner's initials must appear on the commission sheet.

I. Draw is an advance on commissions. Designers who terminate will be required to repay any negative draw.

Booking Appointments

Your appointment book should be visible on your desk at all times. Appointments should be noted **IN** or **OUT** in bold letters. Guidelines for booking client appointments are Monday afternoons, Tuesdays and Thursdays. (Monday A.M. is reserved for staff and planning, Wednesday is long range planning and promotion, Friday is catch-up day.)

1. **IN** Appointments
    A. Be prepared 24 hours ahead for your appointments.
    B. List your goals to accomplish at that appointment.
    C. Review your overall objectives with the client when they come in. This makes you look organized.
    D. Get "Psyched Up"...Be enthusiastic.
    E. Remind the client of anything they need to bring in, if applicable.
    F. Let them know approximately how much time you will be allowing and why. This helps them plan their time.
    G. Usually one hour should suffice unless there are reasons to go longer. Most clients get "worn out" mentally after an hour.
    H. Sharing in the joy of good decision making is part of a good selling system. Bring other employees over to see the positive decisions. . . .share the joy!
    I. Give yourself at least 15 minutes between appointments to make follow-up notes and list work left to do.

2. **OUT** appointments
    A. Make sure you have location directions written on the back of your lead card.
    B. Approximately one hour should suffice for most "out" appointments if you are managing your time properly.
    C. Note specifics carefully so additional trips to the home aren't necessary except at installation times.

(The more care you take noting details, the less trips you will have to make out again).

• flooring	• patterns
• wallcovering	• wood grains
• countertops	• ceilings
• window sizes	• key furniture pieces
• art	• fireplace patterns/colors

D. Bring arm covers or carpet samples back with you for color/pattern reference.

E. Taking Polaroid pictures is very helpful, especially with remodeling projects.

Quote Sheets and Purchase Orders

Every company and every designer develops their own method of writing up customer quote sheets and purchase orders (p.o.). The main point is to develop a system and then stick to it. With a system, things become routine. The design business has enough unforeseen problems to deal with. Without a routine, you create more chances for errors.

As you review the following, note some key points in my "systems for success".

*   Do not give your client information they don't need. Too much information allows them to easily "shop" you.

*   Private label when necessary. Keep good records of where the items can be purchased, but only have your firm's name on the product.

*   Be specific in clarifying expectations of a client. Sell a product for what it is.

*   Be specific in sizes and numbers.

*   For window treatments always note control locations.

*   Encourage your client to review your contracts with you as they sign the orders.

*   Do not give breakdowns unless required or advantageous to understanding the total price.

*   Draw simple pictures to protect yourself and clarify orders when applicable. This is especially important on sectional orders and window treatments.

Quote Sheet - P.O. - Furniture Order

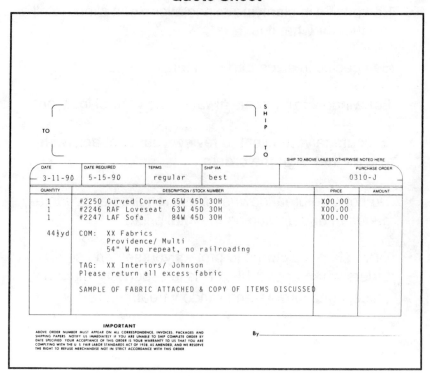

Name: _____ # __0310-J__

Address: _____

Phone: _____ Designer: _____

Quote Date: _____ Order Date: _____

Quantity	Tag: Furniture	Area: Family Room	Unit Price	Extended Price	✓
	Sectional w/skirt	Sketch			
1	#2250 Curved Corner 65W 45D 30H		1,260	1,260	
1	#2246 RAF Loveseat 63W 45D 30H		1,272	1,272	
1	#2247 LAF Sofa 84W 45D 30H		1,664	1,664	
44½ yds	Providence Color Multi		33.50	1,490.75	
	54" W. no repeat 100% cotton				
	Scotchguarded - Dry Clean Only				
	arm covers - no additional charge				
	Ship To				

All orders are considered custom and may not be cancelled unless approved by Touch of Class. This order is considered due and payable upon delivery. Prices are subject to change with notice. Service charges will be applied to any payment past due.
Thank you.
Client Authorization: _____

For orders of 2 rolls/2yds or less, there is a minimum shipping/handling fee of $3.00.

There is a 30% restocking fee on all returned orders.

Sub-Total	5,686.75
Tax	341.20
Labor	
Shipping/ Delivery	Included
Grand Total	6,027.95
Deposit	3,013.98
Balance	3,013.97

Quote Sheet

S
H
I
P

TO

T
O

SHIP TO ABOVE UNLESS OTHERWISE NOTED HERE

DATE	DATE REQUIRED	TERMS	SHIP VIA		PURCHASE ORDER
3-11-90	5-15-90	regular	best		0310-J

QUANTITY	DESCRIPTION / STOCK NUMBER	PRICE	AMOUNT
1	#2250 Curved Corner 65W 45D 30H	X00.00	
1	#2246 RAF Loveseat 63W 45D 30H	X00.00	
1	#2247 LAF Sofa 84W 45D 30H	X00.00	
44½yd	COM: XX Fabrics		
	Providence/ Multi		
	54" W no repeat, no railroading		
	TAG: XX Interiors/ Johnson		
	Please return all excess fabric		
	SAMPLE OF FABRIC ATTACHED & COPY OF ITEMS DISCUSSED		

IMPORTANT

ABOVE ORDER NUMBER MUST APPEAR ON ALL CORRESPONDENCE, INVOICES, PACKAGES AND SHIPPING PAPERS. NOTIFY US IMMEDIATELY IF YOU ARE UNABLE TO SHIP COMPLETE ORDER BY DATE SPECIFIED. YOUR ACCEPTANCE OF THIS ORDER IS YOUR WARRANTY TO US THAT YOU ARE COMPLYING WITH THE U. S. FAIR LABOR STANDARDS ACT OF 1938, AS AMENDED, AND WE RESERVE THE RIGHT TO REFUSE MERCHANDISE NOT IN STRICT ACCORDANCE WITH THIS ORDER

By _____

Purchase Order

Quote Sheet:

1. Always indicate specific sizes.
2. Double check the sizes in the home to make sure they will comfortably fit.
3. Draw pictures to verify arm locations.
4. Indicate whether fabric has been stain protected or not.
5. Indicate fiber content of fabric. This is for the client's benefit in case of future cleaning needs.
6. I always indicate my yardage price and quantities. I find that a larger cost is easier to understand when the breakdown is shown.
7. Do not indicate the manufacturer's for the client. Numbers are appropriate as they can't be as easily shopped as manufacturer's names.
8. Do not promise to meet any deadlines unless you are sure that you have some control. In most cases deliveries are beyond your control and patience should be encouraged with "approximate only" given.
9. Identify arm covers (Extra charges).
10. Indicate cushion requests (Note any upcharges).
11. Indicate wood finishes if other than standard options are available.
12. Attach a photocopy and fabric swatch for verification.

I want to make sure that the client has enough information signed for, to protect me from a cancellation or problem at the time of delivery.

If he says it's not what he expected I need to be able to show that:
• He has a photocopy.
• He knows the sizes.
• He knows the fabric.
• He knows how it should sit if I've done my homework.

On the manufacturer's purchase order indicate:

1. Whether or not the client is fussy about pattern match.
2. Whether a fabric can be railroaded or not.
3. The direction of a stripe.
4. A request for excess fabric to be returned.
5. The manufacturer of the Customer's Own Material (C.O.M.) fabric along with a swatch and pattern number.
6. Your net costs if necessary.
7. Any reference numbers customer order numbers's requested.
8. Any specific contact person and phone number's and acknowledgement number's you might need to reference.

Quote Sheet - P.O. - Window Treatment

Name _____ # 0310-J1

Address _____

Phone _____ Designer _____

Quote Date _____ Order Date _____

Quantity	Tag Window Treatments	Area Family Room	Unit Price	Extended Price	✓

1 pair	Pinch Pleat Draperies 168"w x 82"l - Lined
	Fabric: Montrose/Martle
	      100% Polyester - Dry Clean Only
	      118"w no repeat
	Hardware:Traverse rod to match casing - oak
	Controls:Left
			26.50
			yd.
				955.00	

	Ship To				

All orders are considered custom and may not be cancelled unless approved by Touch of Class. This order is considered due and payable upon delivery. Prices are subject to change with notice. Service charges will be applied to any payment past due.
Thank you.
Client Authorization _____

For orders of 2 rolls/2yds or less, there is a minimum shipping/handling fee of $3.00

There is a 30% restocking fee on all returned orders.

Sub-Total	955.00
Tax	57.30
Labor Shipping Delivery	
Grand Total	1012.30
Deposit	506.15
Balance	506.15

Quote Sheet

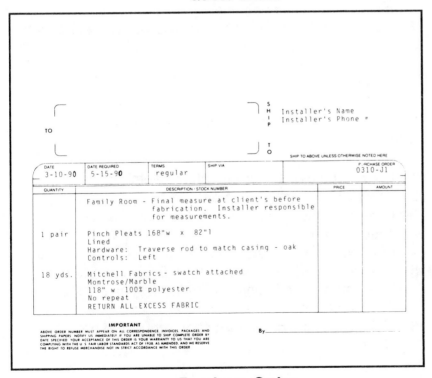

Purchase Order

Quote Sheet:

1. Draw pictures of the window treatment so the client gets a general idea of what has been ordered.
2. Note as many details as necessary to protect yourself from a future problem:
   a. Lining
   b. Overall sizes
   c. Hardware
   d. Fabric number's and quality
   e. Cleaning information
3. Indicate stackback information.
4. Indicate control locations and directions.
5. Indicate any fancywork or detailing requested with sizes and pictures.
6. Do not give major breakdowns . Keep it simple. If requested to do so stress that you are creating a finished product. Ask why a breakdown is necessary. If costs are too high, perhaps alternative fabrics or treatments need to be designed.
7. Do not give information that allows you to be shopped such as fabric manufacturers.

Purchase Orders:

Identify all of the information on the quote sheets. In addition:

1. Give name of installer and phone number.
2. Request your installation date.
3. Give manufacturer's name of fabric and a swatch for easy identification.
4. Give quoted net costs, if applicable.
5. Indicate who is responsible for a final measurement. Make sure there is one before fabrication if there is a flooring change.
6. Make sure all sizing information requested has been given.

- Drapery workrooms and installer often have their own forms. Work closely together to PPP - Preplan to prevent problems.
- Request a sample for approval of any flame retardant finishes if you've added them to your fabric.

Quote Sheet - P.O. - Miscellaneous

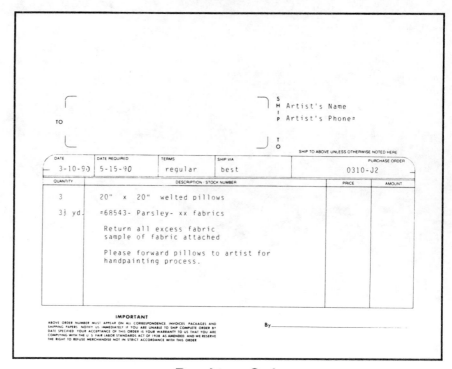

Name: _____ # 0310-J2 _____
Address: _____
Phone: _____ Designer: _____
Quote Date: _____ Order Date: _____

Quantity	Tag	Handpainted Pillows	Area Family Room	Unit Price	Extended Price	✓
3		20" x 20" welted pillows			270.00	
		ground fabric: #68543- Parsley		38.90 yd.		

Ship To

All orders are considered custom and may not be cancelled unless approved by Touch of Class. This order is considered due and payable upon delivery. Prices are subject to change with notice. Service charges will be applied to any payment past due.
Thank you.
Client Authorization: _____

For orders of 2 rolls/2yds or less, there is a minimum shipping/handling fee of $3.00.

There is a 30% restocking fee on all returned orders.

Sub-Total	270.00
Tax	16.20
Labor Shipping Delivery	
Grand Total	286.20
Deposit	143.10
Balance	143.10

Quote Sheet

S H I P   Artist's Name
             Artist's Phone#
TO

T O
SHIP TO ABOVE UNLESS OTHERWISE NOTED HERE

DATE	DATE REQUIRED	TERMS	SHIP VIA	PURCHASE ORDER
3-10-90	5-15-90	regular	best	0310-J2

QUANTITY	DESCRIPTION STOCK NUMBER	PRICE	AMOUNT
3	20" x 20" welted pillows		
3½ yd.	#68543- Parsley- xx fabrics		
	Return all excess fabric		
	sample of fabric attached		
	Please forward pillows to artist for		
	handpainting process.		

IMPORTANT
ABOVE ORDER NUMBER MUST APPEAR ON ALL CORRESPONDENCE INVOICES PACKAGES AND SHIPPING PAPERS NOTIFY US IMMEDIATELY IF YOU ARE UNABLE TO SHIP COMPLETE ORDER BY DATE SPECIFIED. YOUR ACCEPTANCE OF THIS ORDER IS YOUR WARRANTY TO US THAT YOU ARE COMPLYING WITH THE U.S. FAIR LABOR STANDARDS ACT OF 1938 AS AMENDED. AND WE RESERVE THE RIGHT TO REFUSE MERCHANDISE NOT IN STRICT ACCORDANCE WITH THIS ORDER

By _____

Purchase Order

Quote Sheets:

Give only the information that you want a client to have.

1. Manufacturer's numbers
2. Sizes
3. Fabric/ fiber quality
4. Artist's names
5. Installation information
6. Warranties

Give information that protects you from future problems - PPP - Preplan to prevent problems.

Include any additional freight or installation charge information. Clients become very upset if they get a bill later that they weren't expecting.

• Always request dye lot cuttings for verification on most fabrication orders.

Purchase Orders:

Indicate the same information as on quote sheets.

Review information given for furniture and window treatments purchase orders. Take the time to PPP - preplan to prevent problems.

Never hurry when signing purchase orders. This is one of the most important jobs you have!

Measure Order

Measuring and installations can be tricky processes. When going out on a measure, we use this form in order not to forget any of the designer's information which may be important for the installer.

Client
Phone #   home: work:
Address
City

Product   **Specific Areas**

DUE DATE_____

Special Instructions:

Who Needs to be at Measure?   Designer, Client, None.

Key or Lock box available?   yes or no

Date & Time set for measure is:_____

Installation Checklist

Here is the companion form for the measure order. This helps us schedule the installations, especially when you are using more than one installer.

Client
Client's Phone#
Product
Where is the product?

Installer_____
Client called for convenient time_____
Time?_____
1st choice_____
2nd choice_____
Installer scheduled_____
Date & time of install will be_____
Client called to confirm_____
Noted to designer_____

Day before the installation
Installer called to confirm_____
Client called to confirm_____
Designer reminded_____

Client Order Follow-Up Sheet

Once orders have been made by my clients, this form is placed inside their folder. It keeps me current on each item ordered and allows me to see at a glance how the project is progressing. If my client calls to check on a delivery date, I don't have to rummage through lots of paperwork. Every acknowledgement is recorded in the front of their folder. Before I make a phone call to my clients I also check to see that this sheet is updated accurately. It is checked weekly.

Client:		Phone: H W				Designer:	
PO#	Product/ Ordered Workroom	Back- Order	Problem	Solved	Projected Installation	Complete

Problems

Learning to handle problems efficiently and discussing realistic expectations is paramount! Every time you are
communicating with a supplier you are establishing your
business reputation more firmly. It is always advisable to
meet together personally whenever possible.

There are no 1-2-3 answers on problems. Each time I
think I've heard them all or experienced them all, a
unique one arises. I don't think I've gone through a complete design project yet that hasn't had problems. They
either come early on . . . . in the middle. . . or at the end,
so beware. Anyone who tells you they don't have problems is just plain not telling the truth. The following are
the best 1-2-3 steps I can offer.

1. Handle problems quickly and thoughtfully. We try to
   live by a "24 hour" for answers and a "1 week" for
   more difficult problems for our turnaround rule.

2. Abide by the "Golden Rule" philosophy.

3. Compliment your client/manufacturer for their fairness
   and patience.

People are different face to face than they are over the
phone or in letters. Remember the business reputation
Code of Ethics that you must live up to.

Some of my most memorable problems were:

** The time a client said the draperies were unevenly
sewn and the hemline was crooked. She admitted laying
on the floor with her ruler measuring 1/8" difference from
one end to the other. The problem was corrected by ad-
justing pin heights.

** Draperies on a commercial job where the fabric was so
stiff that it wouldn't move after it had been flame-retarded.
The fabric could hardly be sewn, but had been made into
draperies. It truly was as stiff as a board. We had to

steam everything into place permanently.

** The client who had paid a $6,000 deposit on a "Sold" order and then decided to cancel everything at a time when cash flow was very poor. Through preplanning, record keeping, and positive communications skills, the client was saved. The $6,000 deposit was reapplied to a reworked design. It was very important to find out what the client's real concerns and complaints were:

- Unhappiness with the firm being the bank (we had the deposit for over a month and no orders had been placed)
- Fear of being "forced into" something by a designer.

It's important to communicate with your suppliers on problems and also to encourage your sources to be very professional in their handling of problems.

Problem Solving - Ten Step Approach

1. Complete a problem sheet form. Gather all the facts carefully and clearly.
2. Make a copy of the original purchase order, fabric swatches and factory acknowledgements to add to the problem sheet.
3. The designer should see the problem with the client within 24-48 hours of notification.
4. The designer/owner, the manufacturer's representative and the client should agree on what is to be done:
   A. Get it fixed.....correcting completely or partially.
   B. Return it.
   C. Offer/accept a small discount -10% (any more would need additional authorization.) Work toward (but don't wait for) manufacturer's participation.
5. Sign a P.O. with the client on what should be done to correct the errors. This should be signed by all three parties involved if possible. (The client, the workroom, a studio representative.)
6. The studio office manager should have a copy of all this information for their files.
7. The studio office manager should forward a copy of the problem sheet to accounts payable. This should be done **within 1 day.**
8. Complete the follow-through necessary to correct the problem.
9. Monitor problems weekly with your client. (This is basically the office manager's job!) It is the responsibility of the designer to assist. Commission payment should be withheld until completion of a job.
10. If a problem cannot be solved within 15 days, all parties involved should be clearly notified. No problem should remain for more than 15 days without the owner's knowledge and approval that all is being done!

Memo:
Problems are an opportunity to serve and impress client's that you care...a lot..and that you are efficient!!!

If problems cannot be fixed or exchanged, one "should adopt a liberal return policy." As a custom design studio this is only after all of the above has been tried. Every problem also is an "Opportunity to Learn". There are costs of being in business and one might as well face it. I have been in conciliation court several times in my early years and won! Looking back on it all, I never **won** unless I left a satisfied client. Therefore, today I advise that when all else fails ***"the cost of a liberal return is a valuable relearn!***

Remember some hints on how to handle a customer complaint:

1. **Sympathize** - "I understand how you feel" or "I can see that you are upset by this" acknowledges the client's situation without agreeing with their position. A friendly, open, non-defensive attitude lets the client know how important they are to your company.
2. **Reassure** - Fear that you will do nothing must be eliminated before they can talk reasonable to you. "We'll do all we can."
3. **Get the facts** - Don't allow them to generalize. Ask questions. Listen without interruption or argument.
4. **Apologize** - Be sincere in expressing regrets that the client has been inconvenienced or disappointed.
5. **Rebuild your reputation** - Remind the client that your company successfully deals with hundreds of clients every year and that you have built a good reputation based on service and dedication to our customers.
6. **Thank the client** - Thank them for telling you about the problem, giving you a chance to improve the quality of your service. Make the client feel good.

Customer Service Report For Problems

Date of Complaint:
Date Delivered/Installed:
P.O. #:

Manufacturer/Workroom:
Representative/Contract Person:
Phone:

Invoice #:
Invoice Date:

Client:
Designer:
Client Address:
Client Phone #:

Description of Complaint:

Contact Record Date/Person Contacted:

Repaired By/Date:

Repairman's Remarks:

Final Resolution Date:

Customer's Comments:

Note: Copies of original and satisfied complaints must be submitted to the Accounting Dept. to insure proper handling of all accounts receivable/payable.

Client Close Out Process

At the end of each project we use the following - a check-list to professionally close out each account. The check-list should be completed within two weeks from the date the account is paid off. I typically do these kinds of tasks on Fridays, my weekly "catch up" day.

I make sure that we have noted each client's total sales. It is easy for me to tabulate and then keep a master list of all my clients and their total sales. If I ever need to know my top accounts over the years, I can have this information at my fingertips. This is also a good opportunity to clean out a client's folder so it only contains the most pertinent information. I do not hastily throw out information collected. One never knows what might be important five years from now. However, unnecessary papers fatten a file and may be refiled to better places.

Client Name:_____

Phone#_____

| **Task:** | **Person Responsible:** |

<u>Accounting</u>
Acct Card Complete
 -0- Balance
Sales Totaled $_____   Sig._____
                               Accounting Manager

<u>Paperwork</u>
1. Thank You Note Written
2. Client Profile Info. Sheet Complete
3. Color Palettes in File
4. Client Folder Update
5. Problem Client Noted
                               Sig._____
                               Designer

<u>Computer List Update</u>
Information entered on
appropriate list
                               Sig._____
                               Office Mgr.

<u>Promotion</u>
1. Follow-Up Card in Tickler File

                               Sig._____
                               Accounting

2. Before/After Photo Suggested for Album/Newsletter
    Yes   N/A   Sig._____

3. Client Review for Portfolio
                               Sig._____

Date:_____ (Process Start)
Date:_____ (Process Complete)

Contributed by Mary Jane Wissner

System 6: *Residential Clients*

Qualifying Your Customer

To be very candid with you, when I opened my business, I thought everyone was my client. I'd take any appointment that seemed like a potential sale. I took appointments days, nights and weekends. I even sold window treatments three different ways:

Custom/Full Service
Treatment Only (excluding installation)
Fabric/Ideas Only (The customer makes and installs).

Well, it didn't take me too long to realize that custom full service was where you had control over the end result and you were being paid for it. The other two options were spent giving away lots of ideas, time, and teaching without compensation. The point was: everyone was my client.

Today there are specialty stores that market themselves specifically in each of the above areas. There are major department stores that offer all of the above. It is difficult for the small retailer to be all things to all people. It is even more difficult to make a living at being all things to all people. You must begin first to qualify who your customer is in order to make a living, unless you are in business as a social worker first, a designer second, and a businessperson last and very least.

How do you begin to qualify your customer ?

1. **Know what type of work you really want** to develop a reputation for.
   List your likes such as:
   - I love "designing " a custom window treatment to coordinate with a "key fabric" selected for a piece of furniture in the room.
   - I love designing unique window treatments that really make a statement.

2. **Know what type of work you do not want to pursue such as:**
   - I do not like to go out and give estimates or ideas for windows for "shoppers".
   - I cannot really afford to discount window treatments to compete with ads in the newspapers. I do not feel good about myself and my business when I do.

3. **Focus! Focus! Focus!**
   Start eliminating the type of work you don't like to do. If it's hard for you to say "no" to people, start discussing your price for such services and increase them for services you don't really want to provide. Have a minimal trip charge to cover your time and expenses.

4. **Get as much information** as you can about your potential customer in order to qualify them.
   - Where do they live? Try to get a feel for the value of the house without really asking. "Do you know about how many square feet your house is, Mrs. Jones?"
   - Approximately what size are the windows?
   - What rooms are the windows in?
   - Do they favor traditional or contemporary ?
   - Do they have an approximate budget for the windows?

   This will give you the opportunity to tell them what you specialize in and what window treatments cost.

5. **Encourage the client to talk** about their wants, needs, and overall timetable. Help the client achieve their wants and needs by being honest.

6. **Sell services so they'll want YOU!**
   - We specialize in doing "one of a kind" window treatments so that your windows don't look like your neighbors. "
   - We always have the newest window treatments as a part of our resource library.

7. **Sell design and style not just price.** Does your potential client want a special look or do they want the least expensive treatment in town? Don't try to compete with the price wars. There will always be someone selling for less down the street. There will not always be someone designing right.

8. **Set yourself up as a professional.** Does your potential client want to be working with a professional or a "price slasher"? Build respect for who you are and what you do well. Start to develop a portfolio of your work. Ask for letters of reference to accompany photographs.

Knowing who your customers are, enjoying them and the work you do is where true business success begins.

Residential Designing

1. Lead Cards

All potential clients will have been pre-screened by the owner/studio manager. Notes of importance will be listed on the lead card in addition to the most probable method of contract compensation. It is strongly suggested that the designer assigned to a client pays great heed to these notations in preparation for the appointment. Directions to the home should always be listed on the back.

```
┌──────────────────────────────────────────────┐
│  Date:_____                              │
│  Name:_____ │
│  Address:_____Phone:_____  │
│  City:_____ Zip:_____     │
│                                                │
│  Client's Needs:          Room:                │
│                                                │
│                                                │
│                                                │
│                                                │
│                                                │
│  Referred By:_____ │
└──────────────────────────────────────────────┘
```

2. First Appointment

On all first appointments **out** at the client's home the designer should be prepared with the following:

- A manila folder with the client's name, address, phone number and the lead card
- Client contract
- Client questionnaire
- 25 foot. tape measure
- Brochures/newsletter
- Designer's business card

Here is an example of how a first appointment should proceed.

A. **10:00-10:05 Breaking the Ice**
The first five minutes in a client's home should be devoted to "breaking the ice" - making the client feel comfortable with your presence. If they offer something to drink (non-alcoholic), it is recommended to take something as this is "ice-breaking" for them. Be careful not to comment on how you like something (they might hate it!) Gather information by asking casual, open-ended questions. (Open-ended questions cannot be answered 'yes' or 'no'.)

How long have you lived here?
Where do you spend most of your time?
When you entertain, what do you usually do?

These are ice-breaking questions. Do not ask questions such as:

Do you have children?
Are you married?
What do you do?

These can be "polarizing" questions. Discover these answers as you listen and question further.

B. **10:05-10:35 Problem Identification**
For a whole house project take as much time as needed -
1) Ask the client to take you around, room by room, and identify the decorating needs they have as they see them.
2) Ask a lot of questions but give very few opinions at this stage.
3) Glance occasionally at your client questionnaire sheet for help.

4) Ask for identification of favorite items - "keepers" - things to build on.
5) Ask for clarification of what they hate - they love!
6) Ask for input on what they thought of for problem solving ideas.

C. **10:35-10:45 Prioritizing Problems**

1) After a full overview of the decorating/design problem, find a place to "settle", usually a place near a table.
2) Try to establish the client's key decorating priorities from their point of view.
3) If you disagree - this is the time to give your professional opinion.
4) Repeat key phrases they used -
   "I heard you say a couple of times you don't entertain much because...".
   "I get a feeling from what you said that you'd like to use your_____ room more!"
5) Make them think they are in charge, but let them know you are.

D. **10:45-10:50 - Budget Clarification**

Establish the Working Budget for Phase I

1) Ask how much they can allot to Phase I problem solving.
2) Quickly develop that budget with them - list it!
   a. Flooring
   b. Window treatments
   c. Furniture: sofas, chairs
   d. Lighting
   e. Accessories
3) Try to get them enthused about at least completing one room totally. Don't exclude accessorizing in the budget.

4) Get them to agree on a comfortable budget and what they hope you can accomplish within that budget.

E. **10:50-10:55 Present the Contract**

1) Write up what was just agreed upon by the client and request the proper retainer (10% usually).
2) It is good to get up and take final measurements while they are going to get their checkbook.
3) If they need to have their spouse see the contract first - this is fine. No work should begin on any project without a signed contract and a retainer.

F. **10:55-11:15 Measuring Up**

1) Take time to do accurate measuring of all potential areas for Phase I so as to make the most of your first house call.
2) Note heating and electrical details.
3) Get a "feel" for traffic patterns.
4) Note patterns and textures in the room (flooring - brick - woods.)
5) Note colors (Pick up arm covers and color samples to use if possible.)
6) If you are not able to get color samples from the client, pick out samples from the studio as soon as you return.
7) Find a key piece of art the client might have to build on, if possible, otherwise you'll build on a key fabric.

G. **11:15-11:20 Closing**

1) Tell the client you will schedule a presentation of ideas within the next two weeks. Call the

office to check your appointment book and make sure that appointment is confirmed with the client before you leave, if possible.

2) It is a great idea to take something along to be improved such as a piece of art to be reframed, etc.

3) P.S. - Drive away carefully - not into a garbage can or snow drift!

3. **Preparing for your Second Appointment**

The Initial Presentation of Ideas

A. Think creatively, yet practically.
B. Decide what the right solutions are for the key problems and why they are right.
C. Start finding solutions only when you know what you want and need.
D. Take the time to sit down and go through all your notes collectively to help your decision making.
E. Drafting time should not be overdone - deal with the basics needed.
F. If floor plans are necessary, narrow down to only two using the same key pieces in both plans. Be prepared to show them your other plans in addition to the best. (This lets them know how hard you worked.)
G. Take enough time in preparation to "package" the whole look for a room to help the client visualize.
H. Have pictures of key pieces.
I. Have art pre-selected.
J. Be **over-ready** for the project.
K. Outline your main objectives for the presentation
   • To decide the key colors
   • To select a key fabric
   • To make some decisions
   • To eliminate certain alternatives

L. Make sure your client knows exactly what they are coming in for. Prepare them.

M. Do not go ahead with the appointment at the specified time unless you are totally **over-prepared!**

N. All designers should be totally prepared 24 hours ahead of the appointment.

O. Whenever possible, have prices ready so quote sheets can be written up and orders placed at the appointment. (This is more pertinent for second and third appointments.)

P. Make sure you've added:
- A "touch of class" to the room
- A sense of creativity (whenever design work is involved.)

Q. Put together an outline of notes as to your key objectives for your appointment in the order you wish to approach the project.

R. If you've done your homework well, you will be successful in your presentation.

4. **The Appointment- Presentation**

A. Offer your clients coffee, tea or water, making them comfortable.

B. Introduce them to any other personnel in the studio. Let them see all you have "to sell" in your studio. Use this time to give them a feeling for everything you do.

C. Once seated at the presentation area, go over your list of what you would like to accomplish at this session.

D. Spend a few moments recapping what you learned about their wants and needs when you were in their home.

E. Begin your presentation with your best options and your reasoning for the proposed suggestions. Lay the total "package" out next. It is suggested that the floor plans are reviewed first. Lead them through the "plan" step by step. Return to the floor plan, checking to see if they are following you.

F. Indicate value and benefits whenever possible.

G. Indicate creative/unique input - signs of a "touch of class" whenever possible.

H. If obvious objections are made, you must find out their reasoning to gain further clarification of a problem you probably had not identified. Often their reasoning is inaccurate or outdated. Be sure to find out what they are thinking.

I. Eliminate rejected samples immediately.

J. Start building on items client becomes enthusiastic about.

K. Promote the "total look."

L. When a "total look" is put together, send the samples home with the client to be "family approved" if need be.

M. Encourage the client not to seek outsiders' opinions - we're designing a look for them, not their mother or neighbor!

N. Schedule your next appointment together within one week.

O. Schedule weekly appointments until the job is SOLD.

P. **After three appointments you should make a sale.** If you are not close to a sale yet, check with the design manager as there may be a communication problem that can be identified and swiftly corrected.

5. **General Communication Skills**

A. Keep weekly contact with your client until the job is sold.

B. Do as much personal communicating as possible.

C. Be on top of your clients' balance and use this at appointments whenever needed to keep current.

D. Bring a copy of the account card in the client's folder to go over with them and answer questions when the need arises.

6. Job Completion

A. Hopefully, a good client relationship has been established. It is assumed that one's house is never really completed. There's always another area or room to be done in six months to a year.

B. Let the client know that their information will always be on file and encourage their giving you a call later on.

C. Always look for more opportunities. "Do you have needs at your office or business? We do contract and commercial work also!"

D. Ask for referrals if they are pleased with your services.

E. Send a thank you letter when the balance is -0- (even if it's Phase I).

F. Make a note in your appointment book to call them back when they've suggested.

G. Taking a client to lunch or giving them a gift is often appropriate.

7. Final Memos

A. "Time is Money" - the better use you make of it, the more money you'll make.

B. Never advise a client based on more money for you (the designer.) Only advise on better use of the client's decorating dollars. Your integrity will pay off over the years. Don't get greedy!

Guidelines to Selling/Designing

1. **Initial Consultation** - Get agreement/contract approved. Make second appointment at first meeting. Establish regular weekly meeting dates. (Premeasure by second appointment, areas of concern; carpeting, reupholstering, etc.

2. **Second Appointment -**
   Present colors and approximate costs. Client reacts/reviews. Interim phone calls made.

3. **Third Appointment -**
   Designer re-presents, reviews budget/design goals. Client starts to make commitments verbally/quote sheets prepared. (Weekly calls).

4. **Fourth Appointment -**
   Orders should be signed. Red flag if not - discuss with design manager, owner.

5. **Weekly calls** should be made concerning order/install progress.

6. **Quarterly follow-up calls** should continue keeping relationship strong after orders are received/installed .

Establishing Your Budget

This form has become extremely handy on first appointments. It is a phase one budget establishing tool. Together we can agree on a realistic phase one budget. Sometimes I include it when sending out information to a potential client. You can put in the numbers that make sense for your clientele.

Average Budget (dollars)		Average	
Wallcoverings	$18	$30	$45
(per roll not installed)			
Window Treatments	400	900	1,600
(Based on Patio Door Window)			
Flooring			
Carpet/Installed (sq/yd)	25	30	40
Area Rug (Dining Table Size)	600	1,200	2,500
Vinyl (installed)	35	40	50
Ceramic (not installed)	4	6	9
Wood (installed)	9	12	16
Reupholstering (Labor & Fabric)			
Chair (7 yds)	550	750	1,000
Sofa (17 yds)	900	1,200	2,000
Living/Family Room Furnishings			
Seating Pieces: (COM)			
Sofa/Loveseat	900	1,500	2,200+
Chair	750	900	1,200+
Ottoman	450	600	900+
Cocktail Table	550	900	1,500+
Custom Entertainment		6,500	
Units/Home Office			
Dining Room Sets:	2,500	6,000	12,000
Dining Room Chair	300	400	500
Accessorizing	2,000	3,000	4,000
(average per room)			
Lighting			
Custom Lighting Plans	800	2,000	3,200
(installed full room)			

Approximate Budget:_____**Quote Date:**_____

Letter of Agreement - Residential

The following letter of agreement is a tool to qualify your clients. I use it with approximately 90% of my clients. I have revised it several times over the last six years. It has proven simple and easy to use.

DESIGN SERVICES: The designer will provide the following work for the client:

_____

_____

DESIGN AREAS:_____

Preliminary Schedule:

___Planning/Schematic Design   _____

___Design Development   _____

___Procurement/Administration/Intstallation   _____

A. **Retainer** - an estimated budget for the above services and/or materials purchased is $_____. Costs are subject to change upon decisions made by the client. Client shall pay in advance a retainer of $_____, which is estimated to be 10% of the projected initial budget. If this contract is terminated and actual design time(hourly fee) rendered is less than the retainer, the difference will be refunded.

B. **Consultations/Schematic Design Development Services Only:**
Clients using design services only, (procurement/installations done by client) will be billed at the hourly rate of $____. Billing will be after each appointment. Payment is due within 10 days or prior to the next appointment.

C. **Additional Items:**
Certain items may be subject to additional charges:
___Design related installations/accessorizing/shopping (flat fee)
___Overtime/Rush Work (Less than 1 week)
___Supervisory/Scheduling/Receipt of merchandise/services for third party work hired by client
___Other:_____

WARRANTIES AND WORKMANSHIP
We will provide:
1. Professional coordination of fabrics and furnishings and concern for your needs first.
2. Prompt, professional follow-up if problems do arise.
3. Recommended resources that maintain the highest standards of workmanship.

We are not responsible for:
1. Work by third parties not engaged by us.
2. Warranties not provided by our manufacturers and resources.

CLIENT   YOUR COMPANY'S NAME

_____by_____Date_____

I can discuss our letter of agreement easily over the phone. It can be sent through the mail for a client to review. In some cases a client might wish to add their own addendum.

Example:

This letter amends your Letter of Agreement for Design Services dated 9-26-89.

It is our understanding that the $500 retainer will be applied as a down payment for any products we order from or through your company. Specifics are as follows:

1. We intend to spend approximately $5,000 on products.

2. The retainer will cover 10% of our expenditure. For example, if we spend $3,000, $300 will be applied to the purchase, and the other $200 will be your fee for design services. Similarly, if we spend more than $4,500, the entire $500 will be applied to the purchase.

Please acknowledge this letter by signing below. Thank you.

Sincerely.

New Client Profile

This is a confidential questionnaire to be used for all clients (retainer and consultation). It should be filled out with the contract by the designer. This information will be used for marketing purposes only.

NAME:

ADDRESS:

PHONE:(W)   (H)

PLACE OF EMPLOYMENT:

Income Level: High_____ Medium_____Low_____

Double income____Self Employed____Retired_____

AGE:

30+_____40+_____50+_____60+_____other_____

Home: Single Family____ Townhouse____
              Condo____ Apartment_____

Family Size: Single____ Couple____ Children(#)_____
                   Pets_____

Refferal:

By Whom:

Awareness of us:

# of times a client: 0__   1__   2__   3__

"Shoppers":_____   Do-It-Yourselfers:_____

Purchasing Contacts:

Best Time For Appointments:

Sat: Evenings:

Early A.M.:   Noon:

Late In Day: Anytime:

Client Information Checklist

This is a form we use on a first appointment to get information about our clients and their homes.

Family Information
    Employment:
    Him:
    Her:

    _____#of Children
    Names/ages:

    Pets:
    Hobbies/interests

    Type of books/magazines

5 adjectives to describe end result desired:
Him:

Her:

Likes in pattern/color:

Dislikes in pattern/color:

Traditional:
Contemporary:
Eclectic:
Other:

Expectations noted:

Complete room needs:

New:

Existing pieces to keep: (note sizes/shapes)

Measurement information:

Professional Time Log

When working on a long term hourly consultation it is very important to keep accurate time logs. Much time can be spent on the phone.

```
┌─────────────────────────────────────────────────────┐
│ Time Log                                              │
│ Client:                                               │
│                                                       │
│ Date  Task              Start Time  Stop Time  Total  │
│                                                       │
│                                                       │
│                                                       │
│                                                       │
│                                                       │
│                                                       │
│                                                       │
│                         Total Hours:                  │
│                         Hourly Rate:                  │
│                         Total Due:                    │
└─────────────────────────────────────────────────────┘
```

Occasionally a client working on a retainer basis may be charged for time due to purchases not made through you but where billable consultation and preparation time is given. The following sample shows one way to keep track of time.

FOR PROFESSIONAL SERVICES RENDERED:

0.8 hours for the following services:

Date	Time	Description
08/04/87	0.20	Telephone call from owner, RE: Status
08/07/87	0.30	Telephone conference with client RE: Status
08/31/87	0.30	Review agreement; draft letter to client
CHARGES:		.80 hrs @ $75.00 per hour = $60.00

Common Designer Mistakes and Related Design Nightmares

Over the last 15 years, I've observed a lot - my own design mistakes and those of others. These ten keep repeating themselves most continually. For your information and caution they are listed with related anecdotes.

1. **Charging too little for time**. . . misjudging amount of time needed on a project by self and others in the firm. . .administrative time included!. . .loss of company and individual revenues.

   Betsy spent weeks looking for a "perfect" wallcovering for her client. She'd made three house visits, looked through all our studio books, visited wallcovering showrooms and sent for several special samples. None of them satisfied her client and in the end the client went somewhere else we assume. Betsy got nothing for her time.

   The Problem
   A. Betsy was not "the doctor" see pages 242-248
   B. Betsy had no contractual agreement for her time.
   C. The client liked to look and ponder patterns for a "lifetime". It was her hobby.

2. **Forgetting to encourage client to seek less expensive alternatives** as resources. Know when and how to get out gracefully eliminating frustrations for the client.

   We'll never forget the Davis'! A very demanding couple expecting:
   A. Good design for nothing.
   B. Wanting to do a lot of the work themselves to save money.
   C. Wanting to be shown every alternative in the world.

The Problem

    A. The designer should have encouraged them to shop elsewhere when pricing options.

    B. After presenting one thoughtful solution, the designer should have stuck to her principles, knowing her first presentation was her best! (Make sure it is!)

    C. The designer should have pre-sold the "wrinkles" of any job. There is no such thing as perfect. Preparing a client for problems that might arise sometimes is best.

    D. The designer should not sacrifice quality workrooms for price. The client is better off doing that themselves.

3. **Teaching clients to do things for themselves. . .** making pick-ups, trusting their own judgment. . . positive verbal communication!

Sometimes a client can run their designers all over town. I've had the Reeds. I always had to meet her on her time, late after work. She really wanted to be in charge but didn't trust her own judgment completely. I think she just wanted to be able to say she "had a designer".

The whole experience was ungratifying to me as the designer since she was a "Discount City Buyer" and I should have encouraged her early on to be her own designer.

In the end, I returned a portion of her unused retainer of $1500 and encouraged her to become her own designer.

4. **Communicating "wrinkles"** that might arise, making them aware that there is no such thing as perfection. . . . honest, open communication.

The Nielson's were upset because a vinyl floor that had just been installed in their kitchen didn't look "perfect". This factory-made tile, like the product, had grout areas that were somewhat irregular - just like the real tile installations. Susan Nielson expected perfectly even grout lines. She even measured 1/8" differences and shading discrepancies.

The designer should have:
A. Identified that her client was a perfectionist.
B. Shown her an existing installation.
C. Protected herself from overly high expectations.

5. **Promising things** you can't control. . . delivery times etc. . . .honest communication.

Sara promised a sofa to her clients by Christmas. That was a mistake. Unless Sara was making the sofa herself, she should have known that once the order was placed it was beyond her control. Better to have said, "There is a real possibility that it will arrive by the holidays but I can't promise."

6. **Too much "pondering beige".** . . . time wasters. Making quick, effective decisions for a client and getting them to do the same is essential in order to make a living at interior design. The key is effective, well planned presentations!

Many a client has a BEIGE -ITIS. Nancy Henderson was my first and we laughingly recall my discussing the word "BLEND" from the very beginning. You can't match colors from one product to another so don't even try, for example: Fixtures, ceramic floors, laminate counters. The hues should blend, not necessarily match.

Work to encourage interest and richness - not matching blandness!

7. **Inability to orchestrate phase two effectively.**
Being a pre-thinker, a future planner, an idea person and a problem solver is essential in order to make a living at interior design.

A good designer understands that when phase one has been completed, there will most always be phases two and three if you look for them.

Phase one for the Smiths was their family room and kitchen, but as I worked with them I realized that a more evident design problem was the very poor home office facilities they had come to live with. I encouraged Sheryl to consider a complete revamping of her office facilities and eventually phase two came along. It was twice as lucrative as phase one. The need was always there, but no one realized what a significant change could occur with a little planning. The budget was also there or I wouldn't have pushed.

8. **Unclear presentations of ideas, options.** . . "moving effectively toward a close."

Designer's need to plan carefully toward one correct solution. They may present three options but all are correct solutions. The designer's job is to keep narrowing the options, not opening more doors.

Barb Johnson always wanted to see something else. Her designer kept bringing out more. As long as she could see there was more, Barb could never make a decision.

She became frustrated and went someplace else - to look further for perfection. Her designer should have:

A. Given her two good design reasons for each initial option.
B. Focused on all the thought and design rationale that went into the initial presentation.

C. Kept backing up the initial presentation
D. Offered to adapt only the initial presentations, promoting them as the ultimate design solutions.

9. **Paperwork problems.** . . not communicating with the client enough; daily, weekly, monthly or whatever is appropriate - keeping close relationships established.

Clients like to feel they are still important to you even after the sale/closing.

Sally never called her client after she sold her a room full of furniture. The client always had to call Sally to check up on her order. She never told her about a backorder on fabric. She never told her the factory closed for two weeks in July. She never told her the fabric was lost in shipping. Sally's client waited six months for her sofa.

Marie patiently waited nine months for the perfect wallcovering to arrive. We kept on checking every three weeks with the manufacturer. They assured us it wouldn't be dropped. After nine months, they decided to drop the pattern. At least Marie had been informed and had chosen to wait. Selecting a second choice, after declaring the original paper was worth waiting for, was difficult. Anything is possible in the interior design business.

10. **Complete room . . . design follow-through.** . . accessorizing steps by designer . . . encouraging client to complete by self - summarizing the job and completing effectively!

Too many designers do not forecast the need to save some of the budget for accessorizing. There is an easy final step of add-on's - $1,500 - $3,000 in accessorizing if you preplan your budget correctly.

I'll never forget the day I brought out over $10,000 worth of accessories to a client's home. I placed them all perfectly and they stayed. That was a profitable day indeed.

If your client doesn't have the budget or you know it isn't going to be worth your time to struggle for a $200 accessory order, just leave on a friendly professional note and tell them what to get and where to shop. They will appreciate your honest advice.

Client Review

NAME:
ADDRESS:
PHONE:(W)   (H)

Referral:
By whom:
Awareness of us:
Of times a client: 1__   2__   3__

Purchasing Resources:

Project Scope/Services Requested:

QUESTIONS:
1. Did you receive all of the services that you expected
    from us?
    Yes___No____
    Comments:

2. How did you feel about the quality of products and
    design services?

3. If you were to do this again, would you do anything
    differently?

4. Are you comfortable referring us?

5. Do you have any suggestions or recommendations
    for us?

Client Signature   Date

_____

Guidelines for Taking Care of Your VIP Clients

People like to be appreciated. When someone does a lot of business with your company they should be shown special appreciation. No one likes having their business taken for granted. Clients usually return when they know you care!

1. **Lunches**
   Any client of substantial account ($5,000 on up) should probably be treated to an elegant lunch at some point in your working relationship. If the lunch is a working lunch it might be held in a more average restaurant setting. If you have chosen to use this luncheon for networking purposes it should be timed in the scheduling of the job to maximize the situation. Don't be afraid to ask for referrals.

2. **Complimentary Gifts**
   If the job exceeds $5,000 it is recommended to give a gift. Suggestions for this gift would be a noteworthy floral centerpiece for a table. Other ideas might be a special designer travel bag or a designer throw pillow. Something that can easily be seen or shown to their friends gives them a golden opportunity to mention your design services. If they eat it or drink it, it can't be shared with a neighbor or friend one month later.

3. **Complimentary Consultations and Services**
   Often the designer will offer extra services to a client, such as hanging pictures not purchased through the designer. Any excess services should be incorporated onto quote sheets but written at "No Charge" if the client has been a big account. This way the client knows you are really giving a special gift of service.

4. **Cards**
   Should be sent for all special occasions.

5. **Champagne, etc...**
   Special projects warrant special gifts. Each designer should determine the value of the client and choose an appropriate gift.

Breaking Your Client/Designer Relationship

Sometimes one gets a funny feeling after a couple of appointments that something is wrong with the business relationship with one's client. If you are at all sensitive to your own feelings as well as your clients, it will not be difficult to know when this is a problem. From the designer's end it is a feeling of going in circles. No sale or decision has been made or is close to being made. If I am on my fourth appointment without any sign of a "closing" in sight, I know something is wrong. Since I am usually retained by all of my clients intending to make purchases, the following is the thought process I go through.

Personal Conversation Outline, preferably **not** done by phone unless appointments become impossible to make. Refer to Letter of Agreement on page 157.

To be discussed when:
1. The retainer has in a sense been used up!
   Example:
   > A $500 retainer was received.
   > 9+ hours of design time has been given.
   > (9 x $60 = $540)

2. The client is not being cooperative.
   Example:
   > They do not seem to be making progressive decisions.
   > The designer is not allowed to be the professional.
   > The client is in no hurry to make a decision.
   > The husband and wife are not communicating.
   > It is not "fun" working together.
   > **The designer is not allowed to be the professional.**
   > The client is starting to "shop" around for ideas.

The client does not know what they want.
The client is listening to the advice of others.
**The designer is not in charge, therefore:
The designer is not allowed to be the professional!**

Conversational Outline

Designer:
1. I need to talk with you about the direction I feel our project is going.
2. You probably are not aware that I have spent _____ hours in planning and preparing for your appointments.

Client: Oh. Well, I'm not surprised I guess.

Designer:
1. It feels to me like we're really not making much head way.
2. I've tried to analyze why I feel this way and I'm really not sure.
3. Perhaps you really don't need my services.

Client: (Shocked).........Well,.............????..........?????

Designer:
1. I feel that I have been working for you, yet it feels like we are working against each other.
2. Perhaps we need to reassess our arrangement.
3. For me to continue working with you I will need to feel assured that I will be compensated for my design time in the event that no purchases are made.
4. Perhaps we need to review our contractual agreement and make some amendments.

- Listen to their comments
- Ask more questions
- Make a mutual decision on how to proceed:

For the benefit of you . . . the designer!

You should know that your client:
- Needs you
- Respects your advice

You must see that you will be compensated for your time!

Chances are that if you are not feeling good about your working relationship neither are they. I would always advise talking it over as soon as a problem seems to be surfacing. Always preplan your conversations and always do them face to face.

1. After one month of regular appointments all retained clients should be expected to have made some decisions resulting in a sale if the designer is doing his/her job.
2. Each retained client not completing one order itemized on the contract should be reviewed thoroughly.

Acceptable Excuses	Questionable Excuses
Out of town . (vacation/business)	Can't seem to get together.
Waiting for samples to arrive.	Can't make up their mind.
Spouse out of town.	Can't get together with spouse.
Client needs to see the entire package before proceeding.	Designer has not been able to recommend the entire package.
	Client is starting to "shop".

Retainer Problems

Sometimes, even though we have a letter of agreement with a client, problems arise as to method of compensation. Designers often keep on working, without any clear agreement for compensation. Why does this happen?

1. Perhaps we're betting on the positive - sales are down, and surely this client will be loyal.

2. Perhaps there's a built-in feeling of prestige with the job and we don't want to lose an opportunity by talking "terms".

3. Perhaps we just feel comfortable with designing but not the financial aspects of our business.

Example:

The Greens signed a contract for hourly consultation. I provided them with the professional consultation requested for lighting and cabinetry design for their new home. I was paid for my consultation. They completed phase I.

I saw more work ahead. I hoped that a wonderful designer-client relationship had already been established. I assumed they would purchase all of their new home furnishings needs through our firm. (Phase II was unfolding, however, I did not restate our contract. I told my client I do not charge for time when purchases are made through us at retail.) I assumed that since the client had paid for consultation in the past they would either pay for it again or purchase their products through our firm. See our Letter of Agreement on page 157.

I space-planned the entire house and made specific product and fabrication recommendations for every room. The client acted as if he fully intended to make purchases through our firm. I knew my client had wholesale contacts. I assumed that if he planned on using the wholesale contacts he would pay me for my time. I failed to reaffirm phase II's method of remuneration. When I tried to "close" the sale, I was stalled, continually. See Collection on page 227.

I prepared my time card. One and a half months had transpired on phase II. My real error was that I had initiated and pursued phase II, not my client.

Possible Solutions:

1. When moving from phase to phase, reaffirm your financial arrangement.

2. Correct any compensation problems that occurred in a previous phase.

3. Reestablish an honest working relationship.

Solution:

1. As it turned out, minimal purchasing took place.

2. Collecting for design time became a problem as too much time had elapsed and belated billing caused a difficult situation.

3. An incredible amount of hours had been spent.

I ended up splitting a $3,000 bill for time with the Greens. I wanted to let the client leave a "winner". I know I had initiated and pursued phase II diligently. I had hoped for the whole house order on furniture, window treatments and wallcoverings as opposed to the hourly consultation. I thought I was "the doctor" but I wasn't. Deep down, I knew my "patient" was in charge.

Retainer Applied Against Design Time

On this subject, I always encourage a one-to-one personal discussion first but if that opportunity does not present itself, a letter might help to close out the process.

Dear Client,

Several months have lapsed since our last appointment. We have tried to get together with you either personally or by phone. I have reviewed our design contract and professional services rendered. This seems to be the current status according to our records.

1. Consultation services rendered exceed the amount of your retainer.
   $600.00 (Your retainer)
   Approximately 12+ hours (@ $60 per hour of design time) of consultation and planning have been given to date.

2. Professional consultations have been completed to the extent possible. Please refer to the original contract.

3. You probably have chosen to complete future decorating selections on your own.

If you have any questions, please call our office within ten days, otherwise we will consider your account complete and closed.

I enjoyed meeting you and wish you well on your decision making.

Sincerely,

This form only serves as a guideline. I continually adapt all my forms to address each client's account more personally.

Client Not Continuing

It is always best to talk face to face instead of on the phone or through a letter. A letter should be used as the last resort.

Dear Client:

It has been brought to my attention that you do not wish to pursue the design selection process at this time. I was sorry to hear this as I was excited about the house and working with you both. Things do happen, however.

As you can see by my time card, a minimum of ____ hours has been spent on your project. For this reason I am unable to return your retainer and additional design fees of $____ have been incurred. I would hope that perhaps you would find it a better value to proceed with some phase of the project at some time, therefore your retainer can be applied to future purchases.

If you have any questions concerning this matter, please review our contract first and then give me a call. We, of course, would like to see our working relationship continue on whatever time frame is most convenient for you.

Sincerely,

System 7: *Contract Clients*

Contract Prospecting

Designers have always been reluctant as well as uncomfortable with the thought of prospecting. Prospecting generally leaves a cold feeling and is not compatible with the image designers prefer to project. The bottom line, however, is if you plan on increasing your business you must continually be prospecting. The following are some guidelines on how to proceed with this process.

1. **Making a cold call or a drop-in visit.**
    A. Possible lead in comments and questions.
       "Hi, I'm _____ from _____.
       May I take just five minutes of your time?
       Are you the office manager/owner?
       Could I perhaps see them for a few minutes?"
    B. If no, get pertinent information in regard to their name, (key contact person only...correct spelling) phone number and address, in addition to possible office/business needs recorded on a lead card. Ask permission to leave your business image critique sheet in addition to a business card.
    C. If yes, continue:

2. **Explanation of purpose**
    "We work with small businesses helping with their professional business image."
    • Get them talking about whether they have a logo or business colors.
      "It's a very simple way of beginning to look professional".

3. **"I'd like to tell you about our business services."**

    A. **Space planning needs**
       • Is your office space being used to its maximum potential? Get them to tell you about their space problems, storage problems, etc. "I know one of our designers can help you solve those problems."
       • Show them your portfolio or letters of recommendation.

B. **Business Image**
"Are you comfortable with how your business appears to others? We can consult with you on ways to improve your **business look** - we call this concept planning."
   • "I have some pictures to show how we have helped other area businesses with their professional image. Here's where the use of a logo, or business colors can be most helpful in developing your business look more fully"

C. **Product Needs**
"The third way in which we can provide a service for you and your business is by helping to recommend products:
1) Work stations -(custom built or manufactured products)
2) Chairs
3) Lighting
4) Window treatments
5) Wallcoverings
6) Appropriate and effective art
7) Silk plants/planters

"Here is a look at businesses we've helped with products and materials." Expand on this. Show them a recently compiled list of businesses you have worked with. (See Contract Reference Sheet on page 205)

4. **Follow-Up.**
   A. Complete lead card
   B. Leave Client Referral List
   C. Leave brochure
   D. Discuss consultation-only services

Type of Businesses to Target

The best opportunity to make prospecting calls conveniently is immediately following the completion of a sucessful job within a given area.

1. Ask for a letter of recommendation from the principle party. It often becomes a low priority for such a letter to be written on your behalf. To facilitate this more quickly, it is suggested that you recommend phrases to be included in the letter. Working with the secretary/administrative assistant will facilitate this process.
2. Take several good pictures of the completed project to add to your portfolio along with the letter of recommendation.
3. Take the time, perhaps a full day, to market your self in the immediate area that you just completed work.

Small Offices

This is the easiest area to start working in but they typically have minimal budgets.

Large Corporate Complexes

You normally would need to work with an office furniture/ systems company to make a dent in this area.

Townhouses/Condos

You need to work with the developer or management company to promote yourself here.

Retail Shops

Work through your Chamber of Commerce and local developers.

Developers

In order to make a dent in this area, you must have a strong commitment toward doing commercial work. A good portfolio and letters of recommendation are a must.

Builders/Remodelers

It is very helpful to join your local Builder's/Remodeler's Association to break into this area. A strong remodeling background is advantageous.

Prospective Contract Client Letter

Dear Potential Contract Client:

Enclosed per our phone conversation is one of our brochures and a listing of the variety of businesses we have worked with.

Remember us in the future for:

1. Concept planning services
2. Space planning
3. Product design, specification and implementation.

We look forward to serving you!

Sincerely,

MEMOS:

1. Getting an appointment to discuss services is **always** better then sending a letter.
2. If a letter is sent, follow with a call within 1-2 weeks.

Business Image Critique

BUSINESS NAME
TYPE OF BUSINESS
OWNER
CONTACT/RESOURCE PERSON
ADDRESS
PHONE

I FEEL THESE WORDS BEST DESCRIBE OUR COMPANY
IMAGE:

___Colorful   ___Conservative   ___Futuristic
___Creative   ___Progressive   ___Pacesetter
___Low Key   ___Contemporary   ___Impersonal
___Result Oriented   ___Traditional   ___Comfortable
___Service Oriented   ___Direct/Aggressive   ___Energetic
___Technical   ___Warm   ___Efficient
___Professional   ___Friendly

DESCRIBE YOUR CLIENTELE:

CONCEPT PLANNING NEEDS:
____Enhance our professional business image
____Use our business logo and corporate colors more effectively

SPACE PLANNING NEEDS:
___Reception/Receiving areas   ___Office/Work Stations
___Consultation/Conference Areas   ___Sales/Presentation Area
___Other

PRODUCT NEEDS:
___Accessories (foliage, art, framing, etc.)   ____Lighting
___Furniture/Upholstering   ____Acoustics
___Window Treatments   ____Wallcovering
___Flooring (carpet, hard surface)
___Misc. Remodeling (HVAC, plumbing, cabinetry, wall removal,
   additions)

Design Studio Representative   Date

Contract Designing

With a potential contract job at hand, a preliminary meeting is the first step. Sometimes one meets the person in charge and in many cases it is with a designated staff person. Sometimes the company knows exactly how they wish to select a design firm. Other times they have no idea what the correct process should be.

I like to gather all my information concerning the project and then go back to my office and prepare the written proposal. The following outline is our system for contract designing.

- The Initial Appointment
- Information Form (page 188)
- The Written Proposal (page 193)

THE INITIAL APPOINTMENT

1. **Initial Approach with the Client**

   A. Have background material on your work: brochures, photos, slides.
   B. Come prepared with knowledge of the client's organization and determine the character and tastes of the executives.
   C. Find out enough about the prospective job to discover if the job is within your capabilities.

2. **Understanding the Job**

   A. The initial meeting should produce the exchange of necessary information. Be sure you have a thorough understanding of the scope and requirements of the job. Do not try to answer any specific questions in regard to solving the problems. Be sure to gather enough information pertaining to the nature of the job, the nature of the designer service expected and the client's budget and planned method of payments.

3. Installation Dates

Begin to analyze the time requirements as they relate to a preliminary schedule. Be sure it is realistic before you consider the job.

4. Fees and Compensation Options

A. Flat Fee Basis
Concept planning and design specification. No purchasing.

B. Percentage of Cost
Preliminary analysis of the job will indicate whether the markup on cost will produce more or less compensation than the charging of a flat fee based on a preliminary estimate of the time required.

C. Hourly Rate
Consultation Services are compensated for on an hourly fee basis.

D. Time and Materials
Develop a realistic budget that will allow you to be adequately compensated for your time and materials.

- Get some feedback on what they might expect or prefer.
- Ask for time to carefully study which option will be best for this particular job.
- Make sure you can accurately forecast the amount of time involved.
- Add more time for the unexpected. (Remember Murphy's Law page 28.)

Finally:
Try to find out additional services they might be interested in at a future date.

The above information should be determined before beginning proposal writing or making a formal presentation.

The Presentation
1. Scope of Services
2. Preliminary Design Concept
3. Cost Data and Assumptions
4. Written Proposal

This is usually time-consuming, therefore, costly. You must decide whether there is to be payment for the presentation and just how much pictorial and statistical information is to be compiled.

There will be situations where the presentation will determine who the client chooses to work with. In other situations, the design firm will have basically been chosen. Interviewing can become a mere formality when the selected team has a known track record with the decision makers. Know your competition well. Address the differences. Hopefully the client will honestly inform you on how a design firm is to be selected.

Contract Design Information Form

The following form can be helpful to gather information concerning the project.

Company Name:
Contact Person:
Address:

Projected Start Up:
Target Completion Date:
Developer Involvement:

Scope of Services: (Sheet prepared by firm)____yes____no
If yes, then carefully go through sheet to make sure nothing has been deleted.
If no, begin gathering the following:
Specification Services _____yes____no
For what exactly?

To include which rooms/spaces/common areas:

Procurement Services____yes ____no
For what exactly?

Prior resources for comparable services:

Reasons for change:

Is this job being bid out? _____yes ____no
if yes by whom:

Sometimes this should be discovered rather than asked. You don't necessarily need to give them any ideas on how to do their job!

Project Objective/Criteria:

Descriptive Words (5 minimum) to portray overall design:

Color Concepts/Directional Guidelines:

Use of Logo and Corporate Colors:

Products to be:

Specified Only: Procured through:

Wallcoverings:
  Areas:

Flooring:
  Areas:

Window Treatments:
  Areas:

Furniture:
   Areas:

Custom Millwork:
   Areas:

Office Equipment:
   Areas:

Systems___yes____no___open

Accessories:
   Areas:

___Art____Foliage____Ashtrays_____Mugs

Lighting:
   Areas:

Use of Boards:____yes____no
Renderings:___yes____no

Additional Notes/Information Pertinent to Proposal:

Contract Estimated Time Form

Company: Date: Designer:			
Week	**General Task Description**	**Team Member**	**Hours**

Total Hours:
   Design Project Manager:

   Designer:

   Administrative:

Projected Expenses:
   Mileage:

   Phone:

   Studio Supplies:

Recommended Bid:

Sample Written Proposal

The following forms are intended as guidelines only. We are constantly adapting them for each new project. Always submit your proposals in person if possible. Personal presentations are the best. Prepare for them thoroughly and always make them with the end decision maker, if possible.

Dear   :

We are pleased to submit this proposal for interior design services for your project:_____located at_____.

DESIGN SERVICES

Based on our discussion on _____, we can provide the following basic services:

Schematic Design
1. Site Studies
2. Information Gathering
3. Boards
4. Review with Owner
5. Revisions
6. Final Specifications

Procurement
1. Order Review
2. Order Placement
3. Delivery/Installation
4. Follow-up

FEE:
We propose to work on an hourly basis plus reimbursable expenses as follows:

Schematic Design:
Procurement:
Total Estimated Basic Services:

```
Current hourly rates:
Principal Designer:                    $X0.00
Design Associates:                     $X0.00
Administrative:                        $X0.00
Computer Assisted Design:              $X0.00


Reimbursable expenses include:
     Printing
     Document Delivery
     Postage
     Long Distance Telephone Expenses
     Travel & Sustenance

WARRANTIES AND WORKMANSHIP

We will provide:
1. Professional coordination of fabrics and furnishings
   and concern for your needs first.
2. Prompt, professional follow-up if problems do arise.
3. Recommended resources that maintain the highest
   standards of workmanship.

We are not responsible for:
1. Work by third parties not engaged by us.
2. Warranties not provided by our manufacturers and
   resources.

TERMS
Initial Payment:_____due upon acceptance and
credited toward invoice.   Payments are due within 10
days of the date of the invoice.  A late charge of 1.33%
per month will be assessed on any balance greater than
30 days overdue.
```

We look forward to the completion of a successful project.

Proposed by:_____Accepted by:_____

Date:_____   Date:_____

Sample Proposal - Large Project

TITLE PAGE

Proposal for ABC Development
Interior Design Services
The ABC Hotel
Date

Submitted by
XYZ Interiors
Address

TABLE OF CONTENTS

I. INTRODUCTION

XYZ Interiors is pleased to provide this proposal for interior design services for the ABC Hotel. We feel confident that our systematic approach coupled with our professional staff will result in interior design/decor that is distinctive and upscale while retaining the desired charm and comfortable feeling.

We have recently expanded our staff to include the services of a highly qualified procurement and project management professional in the hospitality industry. This person, along with a staff interior designer, will insure that the required design, review, specification, procurement and implementation processes are completed in a timely, professional manner.

We can commit to initiating this project immediately in order to support a December 19XX opening. We are excited about the project and look forward to the opportunity of providing our services.

II. SCOPE OF SERVICES

A. Scope of services will include:
1. Review of architectural and engineering plans for interior design impact. Provide comments and suggested modifications as applicable.
2. Develop and present for approval, required lobby and room furnishing selection sheets. Furnishings include furniture, window treatments, lamps and artwork.
3. Solicitation, review and recommendation of furniture bids.
4. Coordination of furniture ordering, delivery and installation.
5. Selection of all room finishes, floorcoverings, window treatments, bed coverings and lighting. Selections to be made within the construction allowance budget.
6. Selection of room finishes for office area, corridors, toilets, spa, meeting rooms, stairs and maid rooms.

III. BACKGROUND INFORMATION

(Describe any applicable design related projects or skills that you have achieved. Describe why your firm is the best for the project.)

IV. COST DATA AND ASSUMPTIONS

A. Fee

The proposed professional services will be provided for a flat fee of $XXX). Required travel to the site will be billable as expenses based on actual costs incurred for transportation, meals and lodging and is not included in the design fee.

B. Terms

Upon acceptance of this proposal, we will supply you with our standard contract and work will commence. Payment schedule is requested as follows:

$XXX.	At project start-up
$XXX.	Upon completion of selection process
$XXX.	Upon completion of services

C. Assumptions

1. Products and furnishings for this project will be procurred by ABC Development.
2. Adequate on-site storage will be available for incoming deliveries.
3. Scope of services excludes restaurant design, furnishings or services.
4. Selection review and approval meetings will take place in the metropolitan area.
5. Additional approved activity which is beyond the scope of this proposal would be billable on an hourly basis.

V. RELATED EXPERIENCE

VI. REFERENCES

Sample Proposal - Small Project

COVER LETTER:

Dear MEM Building Vice President:

XYZ Interiors is pleased to submit the attached proposal in response to a verbal request for interior design services for The MEM Building. We look forward to the opportunity of working with you on this distinctive building.

Please call if you require additional information or have any questions.

We realize an immediate start up is necessary on this project and are ready to begin next week to insure your schedule needs.

Sincerely,

TITLE PAGE:

Proposal For The MEM Corporation
Interior Design Services
Date

Submitted By
XYZ Interiors

TABLE OF CONTENTS:

I.   Introduction
II.   Scope of Services
III. Related Experience
IV.   Cost Data
V.   References

I. INTRODUCTION

XYZ Interiors is pleased to provide this proposal for interior design services for The MEM Building. We feel confident that our creative yet economical approach, coupled with our professional staff, will result in an interior design that is distinctive, classy, warm, and inviting. Design selections will focus on the given interior architecture as well as the major tenant's taste and stature.
Our approach will be to represent your financial concerns by making design recommendations that fulfill budgetary requests. Design selections will be made that are readily available for immediate installation.

The XYZ Interiors staff for this project will include: one design/ project management professional, one staff designer to assist with specification development; and one administrative person on an as-needed basis.

We are excited about the project, the building and the possibilities the two provide for a distinctive interior. We look forward to the opportunity of providing the kind of services you are expecting.

II. SCOPE OF SERVICES

Preliminary Design Phase

Meet with the MEM Corporate team to review:
- A. Budget
- B. Design objectives and criteria
- C. Product-source requests
- D. Project color guidelines
- E. Spaceplanning review

Design Development Phase

1. Make immediate selections for floorcoverings, paint/wallcoverings, complete accessorizing, and the lobby directory.

2. Develop finish materials and color boards for approval.

Design Specification

1. Prepare detailed specifications for products/ accessories to be purchased.

2. Prepare complete finish schedule indicating all interior finishes such as: floorcovering, wallcoverings, paint, light fixtures, etc.

3. Final plans and finishes to be approved by MEM Corporation.

4. Final budget approval to be given by MEM Corporation.

Procurement/ Design Implementation

1. XYZ is not contracted to assist in procuring products and materials.
2. XYZ is not contracted to assist in quality control of products delivered/installed.
3. XYZ will assist in making alternative recommendations in the event that there are delivery problems with products selected.
4. XYZ will assist in advising where needed at time of installation. If time exceeds 2 hours, XYZ may invoice for additional design time requested by MEM Corporation.

Schedule

This scope of work can be completed within a one week time frame if necessary. In order to remain on schedule and promote efficient decision making it is important to establish meeting dates. It is assumed that meetings will be at the MEM site.

III. RELATED EXPERIENCE

XYZ Interiors is a full service design firm based in Anywhere, XX. We are staffed with design, space planning, and procurement professionals (staff of 5) uniquely qualified to meet the challenge of the MEM project.

Our commercial experience covers a broad range of clients, including federal and state offices, financial institutions, legal offices, medical clinics, hospitals, hotels and retail outlets. Related projects include the following:

IV. COST DATA

Design Fee

The proposed professional services will be provided for a flat fee of $XXX. This includes foreseen miscellaneous expenses such as long-distance phone calls, expendable materials, and travel to site. Full color renderings if requested for formal presentations are not included.

Terms

Upon acceptance of this proposal, please sign this proposal and return. Payment schedule will be as follows:

Project start up	($ XXX)
At completion	($ XXX)

Additional Design Services Provided

1. XYZ will participate in providing one complimentary design consultation for leased space.

2. XYZ will provide MEM Corporation with a yearly "design needs walk-through" and related budgetary information for review.

Additional activity required by the design team which is beyond the scope of this proposal will be subject to a separate agreement.

Acceptance of Proposal:

Date _____

Signature_____

Billing Information:
Attention _____
Address _____
_____
Phone: _____

V. REFERENCES

Contract Reference Letter

It is important to have letters of recommendation from your contract jobs. Professional businesses expect a recommendation from other businesses regarding your performance.

You usually will need to request the letter. It is best to try to have the person you worked with closest write the letter. It will seem more sincere. Ask them to refer to the specific accomplishments you worked on for their company. Also ask them to refer to the "extras" you provided.

Here is a sample letter we received:

Dear Designer:

Your interior firm has been of great service to our company. We used your consultation services for choices of paint, wallpaper, fabric selections and furniture. Your ability to understand our company and make recommendations that fit our image was wonderful. You also understood that we're a young growing company trying to stay within a budget and respected that request and suggested several ideas to give us a polished look at the right price.

If a business is looking for professionalism and quality, I would recommend your firm and your services.

Sincerely,

Contract Reference Sheet

PROFESSIONAL OFFICES/BUILDINGS/DEVELOPERS:
 Kickernick Building. . . . Minneapolis
 Ontrack Computer Systems. . . .Eden Prairie
 Ryan Development (Village Inn at Lutsen Mountains). . . . Eden Prairie
 and Lutsen, MN
 The Shelard Group. . . . Minneapolis
 Traveler's Realty Investment Company. . . . Minneapolis
 Lang, Pauly and Gregerson. . . . Eden Prairie and Minneapolis
 J. A. Price Agency. . . . Eden Prairie
 Gittleman Corporation. . . . Minneapolis
 Mohawk Business Record Storage. . . . Bloomington
 Wilson Tanner Graphics. . . . Eden Prairie
 U. S. Department of Agriculture. . . . Butler Square, Minneapolis
 Ted Kelly Sales (Hoyt Development). . . . Eden Prairie
 Simonson Realty. . . . Bloomington
 United Food and Commercial Workers (United Properties). . . . Edina
 Lakewood Publications. . . . Minneapolis
 J. Patrick Moore and Co. . . . . Union Plaza, Minneapolis
 IBM. . . . Minneapolis
 Honeywell. . . . Opus Center, Minnetonka and Bloomington
 McDonnell Douglas/Tymnet Division. . . . Edina
 Cy DeCosse Publishing. . . . Minnetonka

FINANCIAL:
 Suburban National Banks. . . . Eden Prairie and Savage
 American State Bank. . . . Bloomington
 Norwest Bank. . . . Eden Prairie
 Combined Financial Services. . . . Eden Prairie
 Independent Financial Group Planning of Minnesota. . . . Edina

MEDICAL:
 Grandview Christian Home. . . .Cambridge, MN
 Jonathan Dental Offices. . . . Minneapolis & Chicago
 Bethesda Hospital. . . . St. Paul
 Chippewa Valley Eye Clinic. . . . Eau Claire, WI

HOUSING
 New Concept Homes. . . . Eden Prairie
 Loring Green Condominiums. . . . Minneapolis
 Lake Nokomis Condominiums. . . . Minneapolis
 Ryan Development (Village Inn at Lutsen Mountains). . . . Eden Prairie
 and Lutsen, MN
 Riverwood Senior Housing. . . . Cambridge, MN
 Pemptom Company. . . .Bloomington

HISTORICAL/RELIGIOUS
 Fort Snelling Chapel Offices and Bridal Suite. . . . Minneapolis
 Oak Terrace Chapel. . . . Minnetonka
 St. Andrew Lutheran Church. . . . Eden Prairie

EDUCATIONAL:
 Eden Prairie Schools
 Bloomington Schools

System 8: *Financial and Professional Advice*

First Year Estimated Studio Budget

Costs will vary depending on your area and economic forecasts. The purpose of this sheet is to use it as an outline worksheet only.

Start-Up Costs:
Signage	$ 800-$1,000
Shelving/Storage Units	$1,500-$3,000
Leaseholding Improvements	$3,000-$7,000

      HVAC
      Lighting
      Carpentry..cabintery
      Floorcovering
      Wallcovering..Painting
      Window Treatments

Office Equipment	$3,000

      Phone
      Vacuum
      Chairs
      Desks
      Wastebaskets
      Printed Forms (PO's, stationery, quote sheets)
      Typewriter
      Copy Machine
      File Cabinet

Rent cost
      ($15 a sq. ft........$1,000-$3,000 per month)

Promotional and Business Materials (yearly)
                                             $3,000-5,000

      Newsletter Budget
      Brochures
      Private Labels
      Stationery and Supplies
      Grand Opening ($1,000)

Inventory	$5,000-40,000

      Samples
      Accessories
      Furniture

Three Month's "Working Capital" $9,000
        Utilities
        Salaries (2 people, studio mgr. & design assist-
        ant)

Business Insurance/Worker's
Compensation $125 a mo
Vehicle $250 a mo.
Miscellandeous Services including: $700 a mo.
        CPA and legal
        Computer terminal

Budget & Planning

1. Most small businesses fail to draw up a budget. The budget should serve as a guideline. Since it is designed with the best information you have at the onset, the variances from the budget to the actual figures by year-end may give you valuable information in planning next year's activities.

2. Be specific. Don't set general goals such as "to increase sales for next year." Instead, set a goal " to increase sales by acquiring six new home builders as customers."

Remember that your business should:

1. Pay for your own expansion. If you borrow to expand, you may be in trouble if sales take a temporary downturn. On the other hand, if your business grows faster than the earnings can fund, a banker, investor, or partner will be necessary.

2. Before you take on a new product line, check the demand for it. Devoting a large portion of your display floor to any one product also deserves some advance study. Some communities are not large enough to support specialty shops.

Operating Expense Worksheet

Once you are up and running you will be aware of continual monthly operating expenses. All of these vary considerably depending on your working environment. The following is a general outline to guide you. Other sources such as comparable businesses, accounting books and CPA firms can give you more specific breakdowns.

Month:_____

Salaries
Advertising
Auto Expenses
Samples
Bank Service Charges
Depreciation
Dues & Subscriptions
Insurance
Legal & Accounting
Snow Plowing
Seminars
Miscellaneous
Office Expenses & Postage
Sales Tax
Rent
Repairs & Maintenance
Supplies
Taxes-Payroll
Telephone
Travel & Entertainment
Utilities
Profit Sharing Expense

Locating Capital

Existing Assets

Work with your banker on refinancing your home, applying for a business loan, borrowing against stocks or existing investments. You might want to check into the cash value of your life insurance. Your agent will be able to help you.

Family

Family usually will stand behind family when all is said and done. They will believe in your true potential and enthusiasm toward your work. It is a good idea to have a business plan written so that your intentions are down in writing. This does not have to be long; but if you really want to impress them and want to ask for more than $10,000, it is very wise to put your best foot forward.

(See sample Business Plan Outlines on the following page.)

You should handle borrowing from families just like going to see your banker. Offer to pay comparable interest rates to what they might be earning in a money market.

Financial Lending Institution

A formal written Business Plan is paramount in assisting you in getting a bank loan. A good working relationship with your banker is also important.
Do not be afraid to go to the very top of the bank and seek out the president. This will tell you a lot about the bank and how it differs from other banks in philosophy and service. Dress your best. Prepare your presentation and shop around.

Business Plan Outline

I. Sample Business Plan Outline: (Informal)

   A. Situation Analysis
   B. Problems
   C. Opportunities
   D. Objectives
   E. Strategy
   F. Plan

II. Sample Business Plan Outline: (For Bank Presentation)

   A. Executive Statement...Who you are/ Experience

   B. The Company
      1. Mission Statement
      2. Philosophy
      3. Organization (License & Professional Affiliations)
      4. Target Clients
      5. Geographic Location
      6. Exisiting Client Base

   C. The Industry
      1. Market Participants (Competition)
      2. Social and Economic Impacts
      3. Firm Entrance and Turnover
      4. Seasonality

   D. The Competition
      1. Location
      2. Fees

   E. The Product
      1. Product Offering
      2. Fee Structure
      3. Sales
      4. Promotion
      5. Growth

F. Operations
   1. Capital Expenditures
   2. Operating Expenditures
   3. Labor Force

G. Organization
   1. Type of Organization
   2. Board of Advisors
   3. Organizational Support
   4. Resume
   5. References

H. Financial Data
   1. Net Worth Statement
   2. Needs

Developing a Relationship With Your Banker

It is important to keep an ongoing relationship with your banker even when you are not asking for money. If you see a large loan need coming up a year ahead, it is very smart to talk with your banker periodically in regard to the growth of your business and the future changes ahead. You will seem like a progressive thinker to the banker if you keep in touch frequently.

Services You Might Expect From Your Banker

1. Professional financial planning expertise.

2. Networking opportunites with other fellow business persons.

3. Top rate service when you need it.

4. Extra credit line extension periodically.

It is very important to **nurture your relationship with your banker.** The following are some positive thoughts to remember.

1. Send frequent interim financial statements.

2. Make all bank payments on time.

3. Call to say thank you when the prime rate goes down.

4. Do not change auditors or accountants frequently.
   If you do make a change make sure the year-to-year figures are easy to compare.

5. Always return your banker's telephone calls promptly.

6. Never stretch your payables to the breaking point so your suppliers call your banker.

Cash Management

Using other people's money to your best advantage is what cash management is all about. Being honest with your needs. Ask for as much credit and the best terms possible. For start-up operating costs and expenditures it is appropriate to request terms from your suppliers.

Examples for Suppliers...
1. Ask for 90 days without interest before you start payments. You may get 60 or only 30, but ask.
2. Ask to pay a third every thirty days until it's paid off.
3. Ask for a 6 month payoff period in return for exclusive supplier support.
4. Ask for 2-5% discount for on time payments if this is significant.

Examples for Clients......
1. A 50% deposit on all orders at time of order placement is advisable. This will assure good cash flow. Exceptions should rarely be made.
   Exception Guidelines:
   a. Carpet Orders...Get 50% on carpet only and not on labor.
   b. Accepting 1/3 deposits if client will pay upon installation. (only done not to lose the order when a client initiates this!)
   c. Offering a 90 day payment plan in order to sell stock merchandise which has already been paid for.
   d. Orders of under $100 for clients in good standing.
   e. Phone orders placed with the promise that a check will follow within 5 days.

It can be difficult for today's independent designer to be competitive when many big stores advertise that no payment is required for six months to one year. I don't feel I've knowingly lost any clients because of another firms terms. The important thing to remember is to keep selling yourself and your services. They need to be uncomparable if your are going to be competitive.

Credit Guidelines & Opening Accounts

Your studio needs a top credit rating with its suppliers. It is important to share your credit history with your suppliers. Failure to establish a good credit rating can cause major problems.

I've always kept a current credit sheet available to give to new accounts. Not only has it looked impressive and organized - it also says professional and a good businessperson.

Here is an example of how we organize our credit sheet. We list ten of our open accounts including: fabric, furniture, carpet, accessory, wallcovering and window treatment accounts.

```
Company Name:
Company Address:
Contact:
Tax Number:
Bank:    (include address, phone#, and  contact)
Dun & Bradstreet:
Lyons:
Established:

Fabric Accounts:
Kravet Fabrics  (account #)
225 Central Ave. S.
Bethpage, NY 11714
1-800-537-7787
```

Develop a recommended list of manufacturers/suppliers. Most manufacturers/suppliers have their own credit application forms. Complete the appropriate forms or attach your own to theirs. Make notes in your phone list file of:

- the principals of the company
- whom to talk with on problems
- the manufacturers reps. in your area
- any toll free numbers which might be helpful
- your approved account number

This should be helpful when placing orders.

Lyons - Dun and Bradstreet Ratings

Lyons is a national agency offering credit information to suppliers in the furniture business. You need a good rating with Lyons if you intend to open furniture accounts. Keeping a good rating with them will help establish quick credit with other accounts as you grow. It is strongly suggested that you register with Lyons as soon as possible.

Address: Lyons Furniture Mercantile Agency
　　　　　P.O. Box 3505
　　　　　Chicago, IL 60654

Dun and Bradstreet offers credit information to a wide range of manufacturing suppliers.

Address: Dun and Bradstreet
　　　　　Box 3MV
　　　　　Allentown, PA 18105-9959

Both of these agencies get their information on a continual basis from all your suppliers. Sophisticated credit reporting systems can be an advantage or a disadvantage at times. If you are questioning an account with a supplier and hassling over an invoice, large companies can turn your problems quickly over to collection agencies or send negative reports to D&B or Lyons. For this reason it is recommended that any controversial issues be dealt with in the following manner:

1. Complete Problem Form
2. Discuss the problem with the principal involved in order of need:
   a. Manufacturer's Representative
   b. Customer Service Person
   c. Accounts Receivable
   d. Owner

Proforma and C.O.D.

It might be necessary to pay proforma, (paying the supplier in full or a deposit before they send out the merchandise) in order to get an order going and in on time. Avoid this if possible as it ties up your cash. Make sure all projected freight costs have been estimated so there are no surprises.

C.O.D. is preferred over proforma because this assures you that your money isn't being tied up with a supplier for an undue length of time. Negotiating for C.O.D. payments can be done if you are unsure of a manufacturer's track record.

The goal is to be on open account with all suppliers.

Shipping and Freight

Shipping on wallcovering is generally included in the price per roll. The exceptions are:
1. If two rolls or less are ordered, add shipping charges.
2. If wallcovering is being shipped to another city, costs may be higher than if shipped to your business.

To cover shipping costs on fabric, $1.00 should be added to the price per yard.

When ordering furniture directly from the manufacturer, add 20% to the retail price to cover freight and delivery to the client's home or business. This also allows a small amount to cover any minor problems. When ordering from a showroom, either build costs in as above or list "freight and delivery to follow" on the client's quote sheet and bill the client separately when the amount is known.

Shipping costs of roughly 10-15% can be added to accessories if the actual shipping costs are not known.

When ordering from a new manufacturer always discuss shipping costs with the manufacturers representative. It is easy to get excited about a great product only to find out too late that the shipping and crating costs actually total the same as the product, therefore doubling the actual cost before you even price it for sale.

It is wise to request information on how best to have the product shipped. Accessories such as lamps are usually shipped UPS. Sometimes lamps are better off classified as freight, however, and shipped together. An experienced sales rep will know what is best.

Credit Cards

It is recommended that you accept VISA, DISCOVER and MASTERCARD payment for services. Credit cards are not used frequently, as most clients will pay for home improvements by check, as we prefer. Try to establish whether the client is going to use a credit card before quoting prices and build in the cost of using the card (approx. 3%). Accepting a credit card is a convenience that is difficult to avoid in today's world.

Credit on Returns

Each manufacturer varies on their return policies. Manufacturers are becoming very strict about accepting returns - generally only within 30 days of invoice. This means the client should return materials such as excess wallcovering within 2 weeks maximum of **your** receipt. The 20%-30% restocking fee probably needs to be deducted before final credit is given to the client. Check with your specific suppliers on their return policies.

In the interior design business almost anything ordered is considered custom and cannot be canceled and credited back without approval of the owner. Your policies will undoubtedly vary with your clients. A client spending over $20,000 with your firm should not be questioned for returning a $150 item - 2 months later. A client spending $350 on a custom window treatment that your staff spent 8 hours or more with should probably be charged a 20-30% restocking fee if you would even consider accepting the product back.

One final thought, returning materials gratis can be very inexpensive advertising. You need to consider:
1. The client's clout.
2. Whether you want to nurture a return visit from this client.

Deposits on Account

"Deposits on account" refers to:
- the 50% deposit placed by clients upon ordering
- the 10% retainer fee requested at the time of contractual agreements
- a deposit on a large consultation job

As mentioned earlier, these deposits are necessary to provide a working cash flow. These deposits will help to pay the rent, utilities, employee's wages and all your other operating costs.

The account card will always indicate how much money the client has put on account. It is important that the designer has an understanding of the accounting system. In some cases it can become complex. If you have your own accounts manager, it might be wise to let them take care of this matter completely. A client can be encouraged to schedule an appointment with the accounts manager. The client's account card status should be sent to the client periodically.

Name: Judy Nelson, 515 Woodlawn Rd.   H. 555-6212
Date: 7-17-90   W.555-3232

DATE	ITEM	PD	DEBITS	CREDITS	BALANCE
07-17	Retainer on account			<500.00>	
	Returned upon completion				
07-28	Art po# 0727-N2	pd.	227.68		227.68
07-28	Payment on account			227.68	-0-
08-01	Deposit on account			931.96	<931.96>
08-04	Deposit on account			1520.85	<2452.81>
10-09	Sofa & ottoman po #0727-N	pd.	1803.93		<588.88>
10-09	100% return of retainer			500.00	<1088.88>
10-09	Chair & ottoman po#0804-N	pd.	872.94		<215.84>
10-11	Payment on account			868.73	<1084.67>
11-08	Chairs po# 0804-N		2168.76		1084.09
11-15	Payment on account			1084.09	-0-

Collecting Receivables

Receivables can be collected in the following ways:
1. Personally collecting the balance due with the invoice at the time of delivery or installation.
2. Billing upon installation or completion.
3. Re-billing thirty days later.

Obviously the first option is the best for cash flow and the third is the worst.

If you are a small one or two person studio, personally collecting the balance due is very simple. Your client should know your terms of sale at the time of closing. They should not be surprised that you are there at the time of installation. (This is a very positive way of "sharing in the joy" or being there to note any problems which might arise.) A prepared statement indicating the balance due or having their folder in hand and just indicating the balance due is quite simple. If shipping costs are to follow, simply state that they will follow. You might tell them by phone that when you come, "please have a check ready for $_____".

No one should be offended by this manner of handling an account unless, of course, you have not done your job earlier. You might indicate that it is not really a thirty day world for your suppliers and that many subcontractors expect payments closer to 10 days after job completion.

Invoicing should be written carefully so as not to offend.

As a designer, it should be of utmost importance for you to be paid as quickly as possible for your work. Normally this does not take place until:
• The job is complete and
• The client is satisfied.

Try to facilitate the collection process as promptly as possible by:
1. Being at the job site when something major is being installed or delivered.
2. Getting minor problems corrected swiftly. (A one week policy for problem solving is ideal.)
3. Bringing the invoice along at installation/delivery time and picking up a check.

If you are uncomfortable with collecting monies, role play this process with someone. If you have read a quote sheet over with the client prior to selling the job, there should be no problem collecting at the job site.

Collecting when there are minor problems

Tell your client that problems will be taken care of as soon as possible. Explain to the client you have a one week turn-around policy on problems and try to have answers as to how the problem will be corrected within that time. If the client wants to deduct a small amount (approximately 10%) off their bill until the problem is corrected that should be acceptable.

Sample Statement:

| From: | | Date_____ |
| | | Number _____ |

| To: | | |

Date	Charges & Credits		Balance
		Balance Forward	

Pay Last Amount in This Column ▲

Thank You

Collection Suggestions

Always take the time to discuss compensation terms and expectations before proceeding. Here's an example of what happened to me once:

Example: Contract

A verbal agreement was made with my client's representative to do a design specification and space planning project. It was a rush job. The hourly rate was agreed upon but not the limit on hours. No deposit was made. No contract was signed. A trust level was in existence.

Upon completion of the work a bill was sent to the company's representative, the firm and person who had hired us. They were not the real client. We spent 1 1/2 months chasing down the real client. The representatve no longer cared about us. He had done his job. The company who was to pay was too big to care and felt no remorse in keeping us "chasing" for our money.

The mistake was mine. Always know who authorizes your payment. Always get a signature from an approved authority as to the terms.

Example: Residential

A good client came back for a phase two project. We had always had a great relationship in the past. I did not go over our revised contract with her. I did not ask for a retainer. After a couple of weeks of looking for the perfect carpet and fabrics, the job collapsed. The husband said "no" to proceeding at all with the project. Billing for time was tricky because I had not taken the time to resign our contractural agreements. My time became questionable and what was a good relationship became tense due to my initial cavalier attitude concerning a letter of agreement. Always review your terms before proceeding on a project, large or small.

Here are the guidelines we use for collecting:

1. Collect from your clients personally with an invoice when materials are installed or delivered. I make it seem that I'm there to "share in the joy" rather than collecting.

2. Invoice within 24 hours of delivery/installation when you can't make a personal visit.

3. Make amounts "due upon receipt" or "within 10 days".

4. If an invoice is not paid within 30 days:

   • Ask if there is a reason for the delay.
   • Call to see when you might expect a check.
   • Rebill with interest.

I know of one designer who does not render further services to past due accounts. I have never had to do this, but it is another possible solution. Legal/collection agency services are a last resort that hopefully you will not need. Stating that these services will be used may bring action from a delinquent account.

Legal Advice

I heartily recommend having a business attorney. It is perfectly acceptable to interview potential business advisors. I went through three attorneys before finding one that I not only respected and could accept legal fees from, but also had a good relationship with.

I advise using an attorney as needed to avoid costly mistakes. Preplanning is often more important than using an attorney after the fact.

In my early business years I had several occasions arise where I went to small claims court with my clients.

- I sold the Olson's four new fabricated chairs to use at an antique dining table. They had four other "antique" chairs they were going to pull up and use together. I gave them a picture and complete specifications of the new chairs before selling them. Their fabric was C.O.M. (customer's own material). After the chairs arrived they became uncomfortable with the fact that the seats were 1/2" higher that their "antiques". I suggested several possible options. . . .adding height to one set or cutting off 1/2" on the other set. Both options would have been possible.

  Instead they said they were taking me to small claims court for unprofessional advice. I won the case and they were told to pay their balance due. My attorney coached me on how to handle the case myself.

- Martha Miller called me out to make furniture recommendations for both her living room and adjacent dining area. A floor plan was measured by myself and my design assistant because they had no blueprints. A retainer was collected and our standard letter of agreement signed.

  The first presentation seemed to go fairly well and both Martha and Tom Miller were present. Approximately 8 hours had been spent by the design assistant and myself by the end of the first presentation.

Two days later Martha called and informed me that our plan was off by one foot and would I please refund her entire retainer of $500.

I apologized first and told her that the one foot error really didn't make any difference in the overall plan but I would be happly to draw it over again if she wished. She said no that wasn't necessary but asked for her retainer to be returned. I indicated the retainer was applied against hours spent and there was nothing to return. They took me to small claims court. Fortunately, I won again as my paperwork was in order.

As the years have progressed, I have learned that more ill will is done and more costly time is spent going to court. Today I probably would:

1. Sit down together, face to face and discuss our differences.
2. Come to a mutual agreement - a win - win solution! I will usually concede to the client when in doubt and let him walk away a "winner", stating that I guarantee satisfaction and I want my clients to always feel I treated them fairly.
3. Remember that part of the "cost of doing business" is promoting good will as your ultimate advertisement campaign.

Attorneys want your business. It can become habit forming and costly to lean on an attorney for continual advice. Know when it's necessary and when it is not. Let them teach you to stand on your own.

Better Business Bureaus can be beneficial in offering advice. Consider the benefits of membership in your area.

Lien Notice

On occasion I have been asked by the homeowner to provide them with or sign their lien waiver. The first time it happened I was nervous about the interaction. Don't be. They are just protecting themselves or at least they think they are.

Legally, anyone intent on possibly placing a lien on a job must first supply them with this notice.
It may be given to any client on a large installation job.

Dear Owner:

Persons or companies furnishing labor or materials for the improvement of real property may enforce a lien upon the improved land if they are not paid for their contributions, even if the parties have no direct contractual relationship with the owner.

State law permits the owner to withhold from the owner's contractor as much of the contract price as may be necessary to meet the demands of all other lien claimants, pay directly the liens and deduct the cost of them from the contract price, or withhold amounts from the owner's contractor until the expiration of 120 days from the completion of the improvement unless the contractor furnishes to the owner waivers of claim for mechanics' liens signed by persons who furnished any labor or material for the improvement and who provided the owner with timely notice.

Sincerely,

Note: Varies from state to state. Check with your attorney for further information and clarification.

Subcontractor Agreement

It is advisable to have a subcontractor agreement with everyone you hire to complete work for your clients. It is one of your only protections that you have with your subcontractors. I've had one subcontractor who refused to sign my agreement based on a conversation with his attorney. I chose not to do business with him as a result.

I usually send this out prior to a new working relationship with a sub-contractor I have not previouly done business with.

This agreement is made this _____ day of _____, 19__, by and between (Company/Contractor), and , _____ (Subcontractor), with its principal place of business at_____ _____, for a term of _____ months from the date first written above.

The parties hereto agree as follows:

1. **Work to be Performed**. Subcontractor shall perform work and provide material as shall be more specifically set forth on specific written purchase orders signed by Contractor. No additional work shall be done by Subcontractor unless agreed to in a written change order signed by Contractor.

2. **Payment.** Contractor shall remit payment to Subcontractor within 30 days of Contractor's receipt of payment from Contractor's client for work performed by Subcontractor. Subcontractor shall be required, as requested by Contractor, to provide lien waivers reflecting all such payments. In the event that the client objects to any work performed or material supplied by the Subcontractor, and such objection results in a credit allowed the client by Contractor, Subcontractor's compensation (including any adjustments required to be made for work and/or material previously billed and paid) shall be accordingly adjusted.

---

3. **Workmanship.** All work and labor to be performed by Subcontractor shall be in a quality workmanlike manner. All material supplied by Subcontractor shall be of suitable quality as reflected in the purchase order or as is standard within the trade. Contractor alone shall determine if the work, labor and material supplied complies with the requirements of this paragraph.

4. **Insurance Coverage.** Subcontractor shall obtain and maintain insurance from a company satisfactory to the Contractor, listing Contractor as a co-insured, and shall further indemnify and hold Contractor harmless from all claims which may arise out of Subcontractor's or his/her employees' work, including, by way of example, but not limited to, the following:
   a. All claims arising under Worker's Compensation.
   b. All claims for personal injury.
   c. All claims for damages because of injury or damage to any property.
   d. All claims for damages because of the use of any motor vehicle.
   The above required insurance shall be written for not less than the limits of liability specified in any contract documents, or amounts requested by client or coverage in the amount of $_____, or any limits of liability required by law, whichever amount is greater.

5. **Change Orders**. The price of work or material herein may only be increased for any additional work over the amount of the original quote or contract, or be decreased for omitted work, only after a written change order setting forth such add-ons or deductions has been signed by Contractor, Subcontractor and Client.

6. **Contract Documents.** If there is any conflict between this agreement and other contract documents, the parties agree that this agreement shall control.

7. **Independent Contractor Status.** Subcontractor's relationship with Contractor shall be an independent contractor. Neither Subcontractor nor Contractor shall at any time represent to anyone that any employment, joint venture, partnership or other cooperative relationship exists as between them except as other than described in the preceding sentence. Subcontractor hereby represents and warrants the following:

a. Subcontractor is regularly engaged in the business of _____ for persons other than Contractor;

b. No employee of Subcontractor shall be considered an employee of Contractor, nor shall any employee of Subcontractor be told that he/she is an employee of Contractor;

c. Subcontractor assumes all responsibility for the payment of all salary, benefits and entitlements required by law or contract to be paid or provided its employees, and agrees to indemnify and hold Contractor harmless as a result of any failure by Subcontractor to honor any of its obligations; and

d. Subcontractor shall exercise all necessary control, supervision and direction of its employees to meet its obligations under this agreement.

IN WITNESS WHEREOF, the parties have signed this agreement the day and year first above written.

Contractor/Company: Subcontractor:

by: _____   by:_____

Using a Certified Public Accountant

It is probably a good idea to start working with a CPA from the very beginning.

Expense identification helps assess business errors and direction quickly. Professional financial guidance is important. Quarterly profit and loss statements identify problem areas and force an owner to analyze their direction frequently. A list of categories identified under Operating Expenses follows on the next page. A CPA can easily identify your gross margin percentages for the cost of sales. (In our business this varies a lot from product to product.) An overall average of 40% should be your minimum goal. The following is a list of general services provided for by a CPA firm:

1. Tax planning and business consulting

2. In-house computer systems to provide complete, detailed accounting information

3. Annual tax returns

4. Quarterly financial statements

5. Preparation of quarterly payroll tax reports and yearly W-2's and transmittals.

Approximate costs can be somewhere between $300-$500 (1989 figure in a major metropolitian area) a quarter, depending on services rendered.

Insurance

Adequate insurance coverage must be maintained. The basic types of insurance that are recommended are:

Worker's Compensation...coverage of injury on the job of any employee. (All subcontractors must carry their own.)

General Liability Insurance...covers damages for : bodily injury, property damage, personal injury, advertising injury, medical expenses, lawsuit.

Business Contents Insurance...(property insurance) a combination of inventory and office equipment.

Cost estimates are difficult to project due to the value of the contents and size. Work with a competent general agent to package your best coverage.

In- House Accounting Procedures

The following is a list of basic suggestions to follow in setting up your in-house accounting system.

1. Keep two sales journals:

    a. **Sales Journal**
    Record studio sales on a daily basis. Record all pertinent information: product, quantity, pattern, color, source, personel ordering, total sale, tax, gross sale, LIC (laid in costs), use tax, and payment in full.

    b. **Accountant Cash Receipt Journal**
    Used for quarterly return reporting. Purchase order totals added only when all LIC are accurate. Record: bank deposits, payments on account, total sale, sales tax, LIC, Use Tax and payment. (This is duplicating work but it is needed for more effective accounting information.)

2. Client Account Cards (See example on page 223)

    a. Fill out an account card on any client that is retained or making ongoing purchases. This includes materials and consultations.
    b. List checks, amounts, #, and what they are being applied to.
    Example: Retainer, deposit on acct.
    c. List checks in both journals.
    d. List each purchase on the account card only when sale/order is complete.(Duplicate this information in the Accountant Cash Receipt Journal.)
    e. Invoice as soon as the job is complete. Current invoicing keeps cash flow current.

Accounting systems will vary depending upon the size of business, manual vs. computerized and accountants' preferences. Your CPA will tailor a system that best meets your current needs.

Sample Sales Journal

PO#'s	Customer	Cash	Between Deposit	Product Amt.	Type	#	Pattern	Color
1002M	Martin			4 yds	4	5096-		11
				7	Custom Ottoman			
10-2-89	Smith		164512 D					
1002-S	Smith			1	6	Sofa 1638F	- 812-64	
				1	6	Loveseat 1632F	- 812-64	
10-2-89	Hamilton					Consultation		
10-2-89	Hamilton	9000						
10-2-89	Beck		5000 R					
1003W	Williams			40³/₈ sq. yds	5	9741-Bridgette	Ambrosia	
				7	Install + pad			
1003K	Klein			10 5/2	8	GC-7062	Celeste	
10-3-89	Jefferey		37100 D					
1003-J	Jefferey			1	11	Custom End Table		
1004WH	Woodmont Homes			8 yds	4	A2587	56-Hunter Mix	
1006L	Lerner			1	7	Repair Chair		
1007W	Wise			10³/₄ yds	4	B6310-	Sea Breeze	
				2¼ yds	4	PR0847F		
				1³/₄ yds	4	PR0842F		
				7	Labor Draperie			
10-7-89	Keller	109241						

Source Ordered	Sale	Tax	Gross	Lic	Use Tax	Pd in Full
White Rose 10-12-89	37200	2232		18800 $^{4/30}$		Pd
Jay G. "	37500		76932	25000 $^{12/5}$		11/89
Hammary 10-3-89	160200					
" "	150200	18634	329024			
Ship & delivery						
K.m.H	9000	—	9000			Pd.
Maslow 10-4-89	87440	—		52668 $^{9/5}$	3160	Pd
Becker "	34570	—		22979 $^{9/30}$	342	11/89
Shipping				2500		
S.A. Maxwell 10-4-89	16950	1017	17967	7200 $^{10/12}$		Pd 11/89
Shipping				500		
Harold's 10-4-89	52500	3150	55650	35000 $^{4/5}$		Pd 12/89
B. Berger 10-4-89	26900	Tax Exempt	26900	13080 $^{10/15}$		Pd
Shipping				429		—
Harold's 10-7-89	6000	—	6000	4000 $^{11/10}$		Pd.
Kirsch 10-8-89				5644 $^{10/10}$		
Schumacher "				4489 $^{10/15}$		
				3491		Pd.
American	104804	6288	111092	38522 $^{12/4}$		
Shipping				400		

System 9: *Professional Selling*

Are You a Professional?

I think one of the most difficult realizations for an interior designer is to come to grips with the thought of being a salesperson. Most of us have illusions of custom designing everything possible in a given room. Due to economic factors such as client budget restraints or company overhead or. . . "less is often more", we find ourselves faced with the overwhelming fact that if we are to reap any financial rewards from our business, the bottom line is we need to be salespersons first and foremost.

These are key problems facing designers today:

1. Qualifying your client.
2. Avoiding being "shopped".
3. Considering your time.
4. Being able to make a profit - therefore a living as a designer - decorator.

. . . therefore becoming PROFESSIONAL

Some of the best professional salespersons are doctors. When one goes to see one with a problem, (think window ailment), we usually take their word as golden and do exactly what the doctor orders no matter what the cost. We even save and plan for the upcoming costs!

For fun. . . and a new insight on professionalism:
1. Consider yourself a "doctor" - Recall carefully how the "doctor" makes his prescriptions and how you feel during the process.
   - A. Does a "doctor" ever prescribe medicine over the phone? NO. Make an appointment.
   - B. Does the "doctor" let the "patient diagnose their own problems? NO.
   - C. Does the "doctor" ask a lot of questions first before diagnosing a solution? YES.
   - D. Does the "doctor" make you feel like your medicine is custom ordered just for you? YES.

When one begins to feel that one's design expertise is not being utilzed, perhaps it is time to review just what the job of a professional is.

I suggest that when you have problems being "shopped", perform what I call the "doctor test". The reason I call it the "doctor test" is because when people are asked to name a professional person, a doctor usually surfaces to, the top most quickly. Therefore - when in doubt - "think doctor".

Ask yourself - Would a doctor handle the client/ customer in that manner?

1. Remember - we are problem solvers - just like a doctor.
2. Remember - if you are a professional, "Consultations Only" may be charged for just like a doctor.
3. Remember - "Buying an idea comes from good communication."
4. You need to spend only the amount of time necessary to give your professional opinions - just like a doctor.
5. Professionals (think teacher, athlete) continually practice and polish their perfomances. How do you prepare for your sales?
6. Professionals' (think doctor, attorney) credibility comes from knowing more about their customer's needs than the customer does.
7. Have you done your homework by asking the correct questions and researching the appropriate solutions for an effective presentation?

Key Thoughts:
1. Salespeople are guilty till proven innocent. Professionals, (think Doctor), are innocent till proven guilty.
2. Think "DOCTOR" as a sales tool "role model" when in doubt.

Does the doctor continue to see the patient if the patient doesn't need to see the doctor? NO.
(If your client thinks he has all the answers.........
move on!)

3. Selling is not persuasion..............THINK DOCTOR.
   Selling is communication.............THINK DOCTOR.

4. Always be "leaving"....................THINK DOCTOR.

5. True or False.........."He's a born salesman" ....
   FALSE
   "A true professional is continually working, practicing, and polishing his performance."................
   THINK OLYMPICS.

6. "Spectacular Success is always preceded by Unspectacular work and preparation... THINK OLYMPICS.
   ...THINK DOCTOR.

7. Credibility comes from what you know about your customer's business. You need to know the answers better than they do.

8. All decisions are emotional. Once they are made, we need to keep verifying the selections and back them up intellectually.

9. People don't buy "features & benefits".
   People buy to overcome pain.
   Knowing the pain gives you the insight into the problem.
   Address the "remedy/medicine".....the pain reliever.
   Perform the "Doctor Test".
   The pain of staying the same must be greater than the pain of change in order to sell.
   Perform the "Doctor Test."

10. Remember that all "professionals" have three things in common:

SYSTEMS: Organized procedures for the accomplishment of a defined task. Are you orgainzed daily & weekly? DO you have procedures that you follow regularly?

SKILLS: The ability to use one's personal knowledge to develop functional systems. Do you let your client know that you are educated, experienced and trained in your profession?

DISCIPLINE: The professional quality displayed to enact your systems. Are you as disciplined about your work as you could be?

FACT: Most designers fail because they are not professionals!

They are unorganized and have **no** true ongoing **systems.** They show **minimal skills** during preparation and presentations. They use words like "dynamite, and exciting", rarely communicating design principles to back up their recommendations.

They exhibit **minimal self-discipline,** rarely seeing the need to continually (daily, weekly, monthly) practice improving their skills....like a professional (DOCTOR) does.

11. Buying is Change: D + A + K = R

   D Dissatisfaction....with current situation.
   A Awareness of where you'd like to be.
   K Knowledge of vehicle to get you where you want
   to be.
   R Risk....fear of change!

"The pain of staying the same must be greater than the
pain of change in order to sell. "

12. System..............Seeing the Process.......Note Stages
   A. Neutral........stage one
   B. Aware
   C. Concern
   D. Critical
   E. Crisis...........stage five

Think Doctor

You have a yearly physical for about $300.
You are in neutral.
If you are aware or made aware of a problem,you
become concerned.
When you are aware that it is critical, you need to be
in the hands of a professional to assist you in handling your crisis.

The Professional Salesperson
The client is either aware or not **aware** of the
problem.
The professional knows more and is aware.
The professional shows **concern.**
The client is now concerned.
The professional exhibits skills by explaining why
the problem is **critical.**
The professional is able to share his/her system to
solve the **crisis.**

13. Remember that usually when there is "no sale" there are reasons for "no sale":
    - No Pain - No Problem
    - No Crisis - No Problem
    - No Match - No Solution, you need to meet your client's expectations!
    - No Trust - there may be pain, there may be a crisis, there may be a match, but there is no trust!

We are all salespersons if we're in business and selling a product or a service. You might be surprised to know that of all salespeople only 10% are considered true professionals, **Primary Resource People** - meeting their customers expectations! Where do you stand in the national statistics?

40%	are considered PESTS having little or no training, amateur salespeople.
50%	are considered PEDDLARS only moving stock to sell, close or make a commission.
7%	are considered PROFESSIONALS solving problems with effective systems.
3%	are PRIME PROFESSIONALS acting as primary resources in meeting expectations.

From: **The Professional Salesperson vs. the Amateur**, Diagnostic Selling, Jeff Thull.

The Amateur vs. The Professional

Amateur	Professional
Selling is an event.	Selling is a process.
The "Close" is the focal point.	No one part of the process is more important than another.
Think they're only making money when they "close".	The "close" is the natural conclusion to a well executed presentation/communication experience.
Self-Centered What's in it for "me"?	Totally client focused!
Think everyone is going to buy someday.	Not everyone is qualified for what I have.
Present to everyone.	Know how to qualify "no's"
I'm here forever.	I'm only here to help if you need me.
Decreases trust. Has an attitude of certainty.	Develops trust continually. Is always getting feedback. Has carefully planned presentations, displaying knowledge and skills.
Offers no alternatives.	Offers alternatives.
Little training.	Like a doctor, a teacher, a pilot, an attorney, or an athlete, training/ education takes years.
Not reading and self-educating continually.	Continually "in training".

HOW PROFESSIONAL ARE YOU?

Practice For Professionals

Practice? Practice what, you might be thinking. How can you practice selling? Being a professional salesperson takes practice! practice! practice!

"Only salesmen and fishermen expect success without practice."
Clayton T. Knox, *Birth of a Salesman*

Ball players, teachers, doctors - anyone else whom you might respect as a professional - has gone through a long education process, an internship, and years of developing their professional best!

The following should be a handy list of some areas you might decide you need to practice, practice, practice. Perhaps it would be worth sharing at an upcoming staff meeting. Most of all comes the realization of what you need to practice if you truly care about becoming the best you can.

Personal Salesmanship Evaluation Checklist:

Rate yourself on a scale of 1-5:

5 = Prime, no one could do much better.
4 = I'm definitely above average but I've seen better myself and I want better for myself and my customer.
3 = My performance is average. Nothing memorable.
2 = Learning the ropes and it shows!
1 = Just starting - a long way to go !

Professional Salesman Skills:

_____ 1. Knowledge of the products I sell - all the products!

_____ 2. Attitude toward self-education. (Professional reading etc.)

```
_____  3.  Attitude toward company self-education
          program
_____  4.  Sales goal making skills/follow through
_____  5.  Time management skills
_____  6.  Record keeping/paperwork skills
_____  7.  Pre-presentation planning/research
_____  8.  Networking skills/development/follow through
_____  9.  Follow-up work/customer servicing
_____ 10.  Personal image development
_____ 11.  Mental attitude - Self motivation skills
_____ 12.  Ability to handle objections
_____ 13.  Closing the sale, (timing, ratio to success)
_____ 14.  Listening skills
_____ 15.  Ability to work "smarter, not harder"
```

Whenever you find a champion, a leader, a pro - you will undoubtedly find someone who has had to practice, practice, practice. It's easier to spot and understand in athletics. We know that Peggy Fleming (skating) and Mark Spitz (swimming) have had to practice. We understand that entertainers like Johnny Carson and Joan Rivers had years of practice, practice, practice before making big money.

"As a professional salesperson, you must fully appreciate the power of practice. Oddly and unfortunately, many salesmen do not understand this. Many believe that "instinct" is more important. Too many salesmen put their trust in "natural ability".

Robert L. Shook and Herbert M. Shook
The Complete Professional Salesman

How does a salesman practice?

1. Begin by taking the above questionnaire seriously. Evaluate yourself 3-4 times a year. Note where you have improved. Ask a close colleague to evaluate your performance.

2. Practice your introductions - your first meeting with a client or new prospect.

3. Practice you presentations - your time to develop the sale. Rehearse it, develop it, and analyze it. How does it sound? What were the results?

4. Practice the demonstration or description of your products.

5. Practice your close. Practice the timing, the pacing, the rhythm and the results.

"Nothing will take the place of persistence; talent will not. Nothing is more common than unsuccessful men with talent. Genius will not; unrewarded genius is almost a proverb. Education will not; the world is full of educated derelicts. Persistence and determination are omnipotent. The slogan "press on" has solved and always will solve the problems of the human race."

Calvin Coolidge

You can bet that top salesmen are definitely - practicing - practicing - practicing.

Increasing Your Compensation

There are basically three ways to breathe new life into the service you offer clients.

1. Create a brand new service (non-traditional in your marketplace).
   A. Local market research is necessary to identify local needs.
   B. Design professionals need to look at performing non-typical tasks.

2. Expand on what you do.
   A. Offer preliminary services that lead to design work.
   B. Brainstorm creatively with clients and staff.

3. Plan a market strategy for bidding situations.
   A. Position yourself carefully in the community.
   B. Avoid person/price only situations.

The following ideas will help you implement the above strategies.

1. **Redefine what you do in terms of client needs.**
   A. Continually talk to past clients.
   B. Identify new needs and serve them before someone else does.

2. **Seek clients not projects.**
   A. Clients will return again and again, while a project is finished when complete.

3. **Value price everything.**
   A. Use lump sum contracts and straight hourly rates, both of which are used by lawyers, doctors and accountants.
   B. Never use cost based figures as the only way to price services.

4. **Innovate and charge well for it.**

Adapted from ASID Newsletter - Frank Stasiowski

Sales Tips

1. Find your client's "Hot Button". This is their key issue...what they care about most.

2. Say ,"I admire you", to your client when appropriate.

3. **Handling Objections:**
   A. A business refusal is not a personal rejection.
   B. Don't answer objections.
      Smile and find out why they said that!, "Why do you say that?"
   C. There is power in fact-finding.
   D. Objections are only smoke screens...keep finding out why!

4. Make monthly selling goals.

5. List how you are going to reach those goals. List all potential clients who can help make this happen for you.

6. Think of **each week** as a $5,000 goal. Spend your priority time on these accounts.

7. Lay your month out as follows:
   A. Week 1...Plan, prepare, make appointments
   B. Week 2-3...Present...prepare...present...prepare
   C. Week 4...Close...close...close...close

   If you think this way, you should be successful and reach your goals. Don't let "little things" get in your way when you are going for the end of the month!

8. **Read good sales books** and listen to selling tapes until it all becomes habit. See the Recommended Reading List on page 364-365. Tapes are a great tool to use while driving around on calls and they will energize you.

9. Get a good night's rest before an important job so you are alert and refreshed and, of course, **prepared 24 hours ahead.**

10. **Review last week's goals.** Review tasks listed but incomplete. Are they still appropriate? Have you blocked out time to complete these tasks?

Overcoming Psychological "Sales Traps"

If you can be aware of and avoid "psychological selling traps", your sales production will go up. Five of these common traps are listed below.

1. Prematurely judging the financial condition of the client. Don't waste your time with this. Spend your time selling.
2. "The competition is really tough." The truth is probably that the competition is pretty normal, even though the market may seem competitive.
3. "We have the best quality product." The major difference, more than likely, will be your qualities and the outstanding qualities of your company, rather than the product.
4. "There is not enough time in the day." There is always enough time if you work efficiently.
5. "No." frequently doesn't mean no, it means the client needs to be convinced of your reasons for making that particular choice.

Other psychological traps can be more subtle - such as convincing yourself that your day is going badly.

Look at these traps and ask yourself: **Can you alter your approach and change the situation?** If the answer is no, don't waste time and energy trying to change what you have no control over. **If the answer is yes, then go to it!**

Overcoming Objections

One of the biggest human fears, it would seem, is rejection. To the salesperson, decorator and designer, rejection is the same as an objection! Handling an objection need not be as difficult when you are prepared for it.

Overcoming objections and solving problems requires a special sales attitude and special sales skills. When a client says "She was very helpful," "He really knows his stuff," it is often the mark of a professional who has overcome several objections along the way.

Recently, I had a couple in for their first presentation. I was expecting an objection to the way in which our company does business, that of requesting a retainer in advance for purchases to be made. I had heard that the husband was a smooth, self-assured businessman. I was also expecting objection to our company's standard method of pricing merchandise. . . straight retail, no discounting. In a sense, I was prepared for a "fight". I was pleased to discover that after a carefully planned presentation, based on good faith, my retainer was paid without objection. I was also pleased to find that after a few questions concerning the way our design firm works, the client did not object to our pricing procedures. I must admit I was not as relaxed about my presentation as I usually am. . . basically because of the objections I was expecting. Next time I will be better. . . .because I learned once again, when prepared mentally, things go better than expected.

There are two categories of objections: Real and False. The difficult part is that these objections are usually the same. It is the buyer's perception that needs to be changed.

False Objection: "I really don't like that window idea at all. It's not at all what I was considering."

Real Objection: The client has never seen this idea.
The client is afraid that it is too different.

Concerns needing answers:

"What is it that you don't like?"
"Can I explain to you why I thought this might be a great window treatment idea?"

"You probably think that this is really expensive, but if we select our fabrics carefully we can create a very special overall effect for your room."

Follow these five steps to overcome objections:

1. **Be at ease - relax.** Keep tension and competition out of the atmosphere. The client will also remain calm and you will be able to keep control of the presentation. This will help build trust in your relationship. (If you are not at ease, you can be assured that perhaps your client isn't either.) Somewhere along the line you need to find a time when you too can address your concerns. Developing an honest relationship is the most important thing you can do.

2. **Ask, listen and watch for objections.** Use your listening skills. Watch for non-verbal clues. Listening shows empathy for the client's concerns and promotes trust. Sometimes no reaction is also an objection. Don't be afraid to ask for feedback. "Well, what do you think? Do you have any reservations?"

3. **Create agreement and understanding between you and your client about their objections.** If there is a misunderstanding, it needs to be cleared up before you can proceed. Rephrase the objection into an agreement and tack a question at the end of it. This shows the client you understand the objection. "I'm sorry, perhaps I did get a little carried away. This idea is probably a little pricey. I've got another great idea. May I show you?"

4. **Be truthful and tactful in responding to objections.** Watch your words and tone of voice. Don't stretch the truth. I can't emphasize how important tone of voice is. Listen to yourself on tape sometime. Say the same sentences over again in several different ways. Our tone of voice either excites someone or it turns them off. Don't stretch the truth by exaggerating to get excitement. Being honest is always the best policy, but you need to be excited also!

5. **Learn to observe and note the types of objections you seem to get the most.** Perhaps they will tell you where your weak areas are as a salesperson.

People often buy out of emotion but mainly they want to be assured of value. It is your job to point out the value - the benefits of each and every sale. Sometimes you need to do it over and over again:

A. **At the presentation.**
B. **At the time of closing the sale.**
C. **At the time of installation.**

Watch for the most common objections and formulate answers. Give the client proof of value. Add up all the benefits of the product. Your client can be sold if they believe they are getting good value for their money. There is a big difference between nearly closing and actually closing. It involves the art of moving the sale from an introduction to a favorable conclusion for you.

"Nailing Down" the Sale

You should follow actions that are most likely to produce the favorable results that you want. Qualifying your client is important. This will establish your relationship and generate the keys to your closing. Here are some early agreements to reach:

1. **Design Fee.** This establishes your method of payment and your guarantee of payment if the client purchases advice only and not a product.

2. **Explain your qualifications** and your company's services. Some will be more important to the client than others. Take notes to remember what is important to the client to use in closing.

3. **Listen carefully** while you are selling the benefits of the products and design. Many clients don't listen carefully and will interrupt with unrelated questions. You need to be aware of their concerns and state of mind. Addressing these concerns immediately will aid closing.

Once you've completed the presentation it's time to "nail down" the sale. Here are some techniques that are helpful:

1. **Assumptive close:** This technique assumes that we know what they need. It works when communication is good but can backfire if there are any communication problems.
2. **"Now is the time to buy" close:** Examples are: "Order now so it's here when you need it", "The price is going up and you'll save by ordering now".
3. **Direct close:** "Is this an order?" Very direct, so be sure that you're done selling before using this approach. Precede this question with many questions that will give you yes/no answers - particularly 'yes' answers. The client is then in a position where 'yes' is comfortable.

Additional suggestions:

An open approach will help give you a strong close. Build a solid presentation based on trust and accurate communication.

No matter what approach you take, the question is always reduced to "Are you going to buy this from me?"

Closing is not a simple 1-2-3. It can take years to develop. Learning all you can from wherever you can will help. Watch and learn form the pros but above all. . . care about your customer. . . . for it is the customer who allows you the opportunity to help them every day.

Closing Techniques

I've heard many speakers talk about "closing the sale." I've read countless books on the subject. One thing that bothers me about all that I've read and heard is that it all sounds like some sort of game. . . .like football. The ultimate "touchdown" is when the quarterback/salesperson finally makes it into the end zone and goes for the touchdown/close! Will he get the points/sale or not? All fellow team members/staff members stand by to watch, cheering the team player/salesperson on to victory. . . the ultimate "close". **The ultimate close is: Solving Problems Effectively.**

Ten Closing Sparks:

1. Review your goals.
2. Keep a record of your closings.
3. Practice, practice, practice!
4. Expect a fight in closing.
5. Expect to get your second wind during the highs and lows of the sales presentation.
6. Keep your cool during the sale. Don't show your emotions!
7. Concentration builds determination.
8. Be optimistic before, during and after the sale.
9. Guard your determination. Win, lose or draw, don't let anything knock you out for the next prospect.
10. Have all your facts in order.

Best Rules for Closing:

1. Prepare yourself, both mentally and physically.
2. Double-check dress.
3. Start to close at once!
4. Concentrate on how you close.
5. After asking closing questions, remain silent.
6. Don't forget to get a signature for approval.
7. Thank your prospect and exit quickly with the order.

Don Sheehan, **Shut Up and Sell! Tested Techniques for Closing the Sale.** Amacom, 1981.

Protecting Profits

Protecting profits is a job for all staff members, not just management. Profitability is what keeps a salesperson selling and a company running. The following are some rules for maintaining profits.

1. **Don't discount.** This doesn't increase sales, it reduces profitability.

2. **Make sure communication between designer/ salesperson and client is clear**. Poor communication is one of the biggest factors in lost profits. It can create delays in installation, payment and costs involved in correcting problems.

3. **Pay attention to detail.** A measurement error can be very costly. Pricing errors also create profit loss. Make sure you double check your work before quoting final prices.

4. **Follow up promptly.** Delays in correcting problems can cause profits to dwindle. Clients may feel you don't care and then lose trust. Small delays that become big delays make it far more costly to correct a problem. If a client is stewing over a problem, they'll find more things that are wrong and everything can be blown out of proportion.

Adapted from **Closing the Sale** by Ralph Palmer, <u>Kitchen and Bath Magazine.</u>

Discounting/Pricing Guidelines

We do not promote discounting. It became a company policy by staff consensus that discounting is demeaning for our business. A "Designer's Discretion Sale" is approved for those times when you are forced to discount or lose the sale...therefore "designer's discretion" is in order. Clients are told that all pricing is fair and reasonable for the services rendered. Be price and budget conscious from the very beginning and work to stretch clients' dollars as far as possible. Other sale opportunities are to move studio stock which is either old or a poor selection choice for the studio.

The following are general pricing guidelines.

1. All products and labor should have a minimum of 40% mark-up. Most products will be 100%.
2. No commissions can be paid with less than a 40% mark-up.
3. All pricing should be checked for accuracy and currency.
4. All contracts should contain, "prices subject to change with notice!"
5. Showroom pricing must be checked carefully to assure minimal mark-ups.
6. Family and friend exceptions to pricing guidelines can not be given without the owner's approval.

System 10: *Selling Design*

Design Imaging

Imaging works for me every day as a designer solving interior problems. I cannot even begin looking for the perfect design solution (fabric, wallcovering, furniture) until I've visualized what "perfect" is. I always try to get some design energy from what surrounds me in the design space.

Example:

Location - lower level family room

Things to work around:

> Fireplace wall "peachy tones"
> Central staircase
> Peachy oak woodwork
> Minimal lighting

Design goal: to make room cheerier, more used, less depressing.

Solution:

Step 1 is to solve the lighting problem by changing the door to a full view and keep the walls fairly light but with lots of personality. I visualized that the wallcovering must have a sort of "ethnic - cultural - folksy" feeling. I had a strong sense of the feel and look and went on a hunt to find the appropriate paper. It is easy to eliminate and use your time well when you know what you need. A complete understanding of design principles is a must for even the simplest of today's design jobs.

Step 2 was to choose a color that would make the peachy brick and wood tones look wonderful. I had pre-decided or visualized that blue or green carpeting would be my first choices. I ended up adding a copper-like option to the carpet list.

Step 3 was to find fabrics to fill in the gaps. It was also an easier solution to search for fabrics last -
- less square footage coverage
- more available choices

Visualization is a must in being a good designer. The time taken to methodically eliminate options - to creatively visualize at the onset of the project keeps you from countless wasted hours down the road.

Selling Consultations

1. When setting up the appointment with the client suggest that they **take the time** to do the following before you come out:
   A. Do a walk-through of the house, jotting down questions and concerns for each room.
   B. Pull out pictures or "rare miscellany" for your professional input as to its potential use.
   C. Pre-think what they hope to solve through the consultation.

2. At the **onset of the appointment** verify that this is a general consultation with an hourly fee.
   A. Take into account traveling time but handle fairly at your own discretion. (Some designers will split the fee for traveling time)
   B. Handle a consultation session just as that. Do not try to turn it into a potential 'sales' job until the very end if the situation is a possibility.

3. Begin by letting them take you around and discuss their concerns. **Don't be too quick to jump in with solutions**. Let them talk about all the problems from room to room first...then go back and address each one after you've had a chance to absorb and hear all they have to say. **It is often important to keep the client on track as they tend to ramble. Do not get into miscellaneous chit chat.**

4. Make it clear that with general consultations we throw out a lot of ideas, some better than others. It is their choice which ones to accept and reject. Always end with what you would do if you were them and try to consult in that manner......**putting yourself in their shoes!**
   Discussion:
   Lifestyle...Probable Budget

5. Suggest they take notes so they'll remember everything.

6. Don't be afraid to give them local sources. They'll appreciate you for it. Don't be afraid to recommend discount stores for bedspreads for kids, etc.

7. Try and leave some quick sketches or floor plans for them. People always feel like they are getting their money's worth when they have something tangible in their hands.

8. Get a feeling for whether or not they are a "DIYer" (do-it yourselfer) or Bargain Hunter or "Wholesaler". If they are, leave them alone to their own resources. You're better off staying out of it.

9. If there is potential work/sales for you, have them pay for the consultation given. Note: See contract and make appropriate decision.

10. **Consultations requiring space planning:**
   A. Try to do as much right there on the job with them.
   B. Talk and sketch it through with them until you both finally agree on the most likely solution.
   C. If actual accurate drawings/floorplans are needed, be sure to give the client the **"two good reasons"** approach to spending more consultation hours for further drafting solutions.
      • Two or three floorplans should be given for addition or remodeling bids. Plans can only be done effectively by "playing around" with the actual square footage.
      • The size of the job warrants more time for measuring needs.
   D. All billable floor plans and space planning consultations must have a contract signed with the client to assure an accurate understanding of the scope of the project.

1) *Example:*

   1 1/2 hour on-site design problem input with client.

   3 hour design planning and drafting.

   1 hour presentation with client.

   "5-6" hour maximum invoice........$360.

2) Get a 50% deposit at the time of the contract signing. Balance due upon completion.

3) Identify what the plan will include:
   a. 3-4 plans.....with measurements.
   b. Recommended materials.
   c. Recommended products/colors.

4) Identify what the plan will not include:
   a. Will not include costs.
   b. Will not include samples/ product recommendations.
   c. Will not be done on a blue print format/ paper, unless upcharges are agreed upon.

11. **Additional Suggestions**
   A. Recap the positive points you have given the client.
   B. Recap the suggestions you have made that have saved them time and money.
   C. Ask for their response to your consultation.
   "Were you pleased with this consultation?"
   "Has this consultation given you the answers to your questions satisfactorily?"
   D. Ask for referrals when appropriate.
   "I'm glad you are pleased with this consultation. Please take an extra card of mine and refer our services to someone else in need."
   E. Suggest that they call you again when another consultation might be appropriate on the project.

Selling Wallcovering

1. Visit the home first, if possible.

2. Note existing patterns within the area.....patterns that are permanent to the job.

   Example:

Walls	architectural lines, texture, patterns
Window Treatments	texture, hardware lines, color
Floors	patterns, colors, shapes,scale
Adjacent Wallcoverings	patterns, colors, shapes,scale
Fabrics/Upholstery	patterns, colors, texture
Fireplaces	patterns, color, texture

3. Pick up any appropriate samples available.

4. Draw a rough floorplan sketch of how the rooms relate to each other.

5. Come to a semi-conclusion of what type/color tones of paper should be sought before you leave the house. Take a quiet moment to step back and reflect.

6. If you have any strong feeling toward perhaps dark wallcovering, strings, etc. check it out with your client before leaving so you don't go off on a wrong track, especially when you have an entire floor or house to do.

7. **Note client requests on past likes and dislikes.** Find out about their maintenance expectation level. Ask them to give you adjectives for each room. How do they want to "feel" when they enter each room. **Kitchen:** warm, friendly, spacious **Dining Room:** elegant, airy

8. **Pencil in your plan of attack on your floorplan.**
   Remember to consider the "basic five" pattern approach. If the appropriate scale is used, (large, medium and small) and the appropriate value combinations, (light, medium hue and dark), then the "basic five" patterns can work together in converging areas.

   Think like you were putting together a new outfit.......with five separates: skirt, jacket, blouse, scarf, and sweater. If the textures are compatible, the scales varied and compatible, and the color balance blends in a striking manner, then up to five different patterns can be exciting.

   A. **Solids**..in overall feeling/impression
      Moires, grasscloths, strings, and textured vinyls are examples of solid-like papers.

   B. **Stripes**
      Often stripes are mixed with floral patterns. They can be muted or strongly contrasted patterns. There are contemporary primary colored, crisp, clean stripes and also very traditional rich, warm, cozy stripes.

   C. **Geometrics**
      Geometrics can be large or small in scale. They can be two toned or multi colored plaids. Depending on the colorations they can vary from more contemporary-like or traditional.

   D. **Overall Patterns**
      Overall patterns tend to be more floral-like. They can have many colors such as the English Cabbage Patch florals that Waverly has made popular or muted "tone on tone" subtle English reproductions suitable for stately foyers. Mini prints can be "overalls" but very small in scale.

E. **Medallion Patterns**
   The simple fleur-de-lis pattern is most representative of the medallion pattern. A more contemporary version could be a geometric shaped mini print. A more traditional version of this pattern might be a large scale two colored medallion-like documentary such as a blue and white wedgewood pattern.

F. A **combination** of two or more of the above.
   We all are aware of the many exceptions or questionable patterns that will arise. Chances are that they will fit into this category. For planning purposes just realize that more than five patterns can be very confusing. Eliminate another from above when making a selection that is a combination pattern.

   *Note: The author has been instrumental in the development of this wallcovering selection system. It is presently being used by Black & Decker in their book, Decorating With Paint & Wallcovering, Cy DeCosse Publishing 1988.

9. **Start with a "key pattern."**

   Where do you need it? The dining room walls? Maybe there already is a "key pattern" in close proximity. Perhaps draperies or sofa patterns in the living room are prominent enough to be considered "key".

   Think about standing in the foyer/hallway and looking into each room. Mentally stand in each room. How many papers can you see? How are they all going to flow together?

   Remember to think like you are getting dressed. Would you wear all those patterns together? If you couldn't be comfortable with similar combinations on your body for a day, chances are it would drive you up a wall in your home within one week.

10. **Finally...it is a waste of time to start looking for wallcovering unless you know what you are looking for.**

   You are wasting your time and more important-ly....losing money.

   Your time is either...your salary or no salary. Your choice!
   See page 252 Increasing Your Compensation

11. Checklist before starting:

   Pattern Type:
   Solid-like
   Stripes
   Geometric
   Overall
   Medallion
   Combination

Value:	**Scale:**
Light	Small
Medium	Medium
Dark	Large

12. Once you know what you are looking for, start going through the books and give yourself a maximum of one-half hour or one hour. Make no ultimate selections but start marking pages of possibilities. Don't forget to be aware of the cost of the papers, keeping the budget in mind. If a paper is really right, how-ever, most people will realize it and pay what it costs. Also be aware of the paper quality: vinyl, fabric back, paperback vinyls, vinyl coated and just wallpaper. Know the differences and when to rec-ommend what.

Stack the books in piles arranged like your floor plan. Eliminate as you go along when a better option comes along. When you get close to your time limit, go through each pile and eliminate down to no more than three in a pile. Stack them and walk away from the project till the next day. Then start fresh and review. Layout your best options.

Present your options in a floor plan like manner.

You are now ready to meet with your client.

13. When presenting begin with an introduction of why and how you are going to proceed/present. Make the client feel comfortable and let them know that if they strongly dislike a pattern when they see it, to speak up . When a pattern gets eliminated ask, " What was it that you disliked about the paper?" This helps you readjust quickly and understand your client better.

14. It is often hard to know whether or not to ask for feedback as you are presenting. It depends on the client and the length of the presentation.

15. Let them go home with no more than three options for a key area. Always back up your selections with design principles as to why they were originally selected.

16. When planned carefully to begin with, and when you are truly the designer/decorator.....not a wallcovering clerk..........you become an authority.......therefore eliminating costly time-wasting redos.

This step-by-step system is the way to make money selling wallcovering. For me it's the only way!

Here are some final memos when it comes to wall-covering.

1. When requesting larger memo samples - allow enough time for mailing.
2. Always check for correct pattern number and color, and matching run numbers
3. Make sure the wall surfaces have been prepared properly.
4. Know how and when to identify defective goods.
5. Always use correct adhesives.
6. Exercise good judgment. If a problem is detected, stop work immediately. One can usually detect a problem after 2-3 strips. Explain the problem to your client.
7. Understand that colorfastness may be a problem. No manufacturer guarantees against fading.
8. Explain to clients that darker wallcoverings usually show seams more readily.
9. Explain that coordinating fabrics does not mean matching.
10. Make sure that installers are experienced and responsible. I always have held installers responsible for all measurements.
11. Understand that metric papers require different rollage amounts than American.
12. Allow for pattern repeats when measuring for paper.
13. Selling custom colored paper can be an advantage in becoming distinctive. (8-12 rolls is usually the minimum amount of rollage required.)
14. Recommend liners for problem walls.

Selling Flooring

1. Assess flooring needs by **asking a lot of questions.**
   A. Discover likes, dislikes and priorities
      - Color/the Look
      - Quality and maintenance needs
      - Price
        It is wise to recommend more money be put into high traffic areas.
   B. Make positive recommendations and get immediate feedback.

2. Eliminate price comparison shopping. **Private labeling** helps facilitate this.

3. Match comparison pricing only if needed to keep the client and minimum profit margin is maintained.

4. Sell service, service, service.

5. **Padding**...It is often not necessary to get into great detail over padding. It is recommended that one standard pad such as a 3/8" rebond is stocked and used. However, it is important to check with the client to note if this is satisfactory. Give them two good reasons for your recommendation.
   A. It has become a national standard in the business.
   B. It will hold up well for the life of the carpet.

   If clients want a "cushier" feel, perhaps they should increase to 9/16" pad. For berbers, a solid urethane pad is preferable. When in doubt, check with your carpet installer.

6. **Technical information**...It is important that you know your product. When a client requests additional information, rely on your supplier for more complete details. Remember, shoppers become almost instant experts - a little knowledge can be a dangerous thing so sell your expertise as designer.

7. Maintenance information...Check with your supplier.

8. **Hard surface** options:
   A. Ceramic/ Quarry Tile
   B. Wood
   C. Vinyl
   D. Marble, Slate, etc.

Know the advantages and disadvantages of each.

Fabrication Guidelines

1. Beds must be measured for custom bedspreads. **Measurements** should be taken with appropriate bedding on and the final floor surface taken into account.

2. Notations should be made on all P.O.s if scraps are to be returned to the client for pillows, etc. **Be careful how much waste you return.**

3. Guidelines for upholstery workroom PO's are as follows:
   A. Note "as is" if no changes are needed.
   B. Note changes and alterations carefully.
   C. All POs should be signed by the client/designer/ upholsterer (white to client, yellow to designer, pink to upholsterer).
   D. Deliveries are scheduled between the workroom and Studio Manager.

4. **All drapery jobs will be measured.**
   A. Be on-site with the installer for all final measurements of window treatments.
   B. Be clear about expectations.
   C. Sell "wrinkles" with the client - how fabric will hang, etc.
   D. Make sure your P.O.s have all details necessary:
      1) Fabric cuttings
      2) Pictures
      3) Client expectations: "client very fussy"
   E. Be present at the "tail end " of all installations to fuss a little with the end result and finally "resell" the job.
   F. Notations of all measurements must be in client's folder.

   Don't forget to note:
   1) Flooring/carpet - new
   2) Hardware - new/old
   3) Clearance space for stacking/extensions
   4) Heat sources

G. General mounting clearances installers will follow:

Draperies	mounted 1 1/2" above casing 3/8" - 1/2" above floor clearance 1/2" - 2" below apron
Verticals	same as above (add 1 1/2" - 3" to each side)
Mini blinds	1/4" clearance on all sides if possible
Roman shades	1 1/2" - 3" each side and bottom, 1" above casing

H. All yardage requirements and costs will be given by workroom doing the work (drapery/upholstery/bedspreads) before information is given to client and quote sheet completed. This information should be written on the back side of the yellow copy of the quote sheet or on the pink copy of quote sheet. Note all laid in costs.

I. When quotes are not firm indicate this on the quote sheet by quotes i.e. "$50.00" around the price and noting that you will get back with the final verifications. Orders can still be processed however, if the client is informed that price is subject to change.

Note: All of our client quote sheets say: "Prices subject to change with notice". This is for our protection. This should of course be done promptly. One week prior to installation may be too late for the average client.

Window Treatment Guidelines

Unpatterned Fabric

1. Finished width x fullness (3 x for sheers, 2 1/2 for medium -heavy). Add 3" for each side hem.
2. Total width divided by fabric width (ie. 45", 54") equals number of fabric widths (round up).
3. Finished length plus hems and heading allowance (20") equals cut length.
4. Number of fabric widths x cut length equals total length in inches.
5. Total length in inches divided by 36 equals total yardage.

> *Example:*
> 60" x 2.5 = 150" + 20" (hem & headings) = 170"
> 170 divided by 45 (fabric width) = 3.70 (round up to 4 widths)
> 4 x 81" (cut length) = 324
> 324" divided by 36 = total yardage, 9 yards

Patterned Fabric

1. Finished width x fullness + side hems.
2. Total width divided by fabric width (usable fabric) equals number of fabric widths.
3. Cut length divided by repeat equals number of repeats needed for each cut length (round up).
4. Number of repeats needed for each cut length x repeat equals adjusted cut length.
5. Adjusted cut length x number of fabric widths equals total length in inches.
6. Total length in inches divided by 36 equals total yardage.

> *Example:*
> 60" X 2.5 = 150 + 3" = 153
> 153 divided by 45 = 3.4 (round up to 4)
> 81" (cut length) divided by 15" (repeat) = 5.40 (round up to 6) = number of repeats needed for each cut length.
> 6 x 15" = 90" (adjusted cut length)
> 90" x 4 = 360
> 360 divided by 36 = 10 yards.

118" Fabric

1. 118" fabric is usually railroaded, using selvage to selvage width for the length, enabling you to produce seamless draperies.

2. Yardage Formula for railroading:

> *Example:*
> 1 pair: 160" w (finished width) x 85"l (finished length)
>> 160
>> x3
>> 480
>> +12"(4 side hems)
>> 492" divided by 36 (1 yard) =13 5/8 yards
>
> Now to determine the number of widths, as most workrooms charge per width,
> *Example:*
> 492" divided by 48" (average width of most fabrics) = 10 1/4 widths

3. Wide Width Fabric Fabricated by the Width Formula: *Note finished length.

> *Example:*
> 1 pair 160" w (finished length) x 120" l (finished width)
>> 160
>> x3
>> 480"
>> +12" (4 side hems)
>> 492" divided by 118" = 4.16 = 4 widths x 140" (cut length) = 560" divided by 36"=15 5/8 yds.

Drapery Stamp

I heard a true story about a beginning designer who closed a drapery sale and drove off quite pleased with herself until she realized that she forgot to add the cost of the lining. She quickly refigured and drove back to the client's house. "No problem," said the client, "mistakes happen." Upon arriving home she decided to recheck all her figures more thoroughly. It was then she realized she'd forgotten to add the price of the RODS! She called her client from her home/office and apologetically explained that once again she'd forgotten to include rods and that there would be a slight increase.

The designer was then writing up her purchase order for her workroom when the workroom pointed out that there would be extra charges for "fancy" trimming planned. Guess who got the job after the client was called with the new found upcharges? Yes, it is a true story and my new client was ready to start working with a professional.

The following have been important trade rules that have worked best for me in eliminating some problems that go along with window treatments.

I had a large rubber stamp made for myself and my design staff to assist in the pricing of draperies. There is a lot to remember.

#___	YD.	_____
#___	YD.	_____
#___	LINING	_____
#___	W. LABOR	_____
	INSTALL	_____
	RODS	_____
	TRIP CHG.	_____
___	MISC.	_____
	TOTAL	_____

1. State that the designer's preliminary measurements are **subject to change with notification**, once the installer has measured and the workroom has approved the order.

2. Make sure your contract states - "Subject to change with notice."

3. Use professional installers and workrooms for final measurements. This protects you and is well worth the extra costs.

4. Give yourself **24 hours** to give a firm price to a client. Don't pressure yourself to do it at the job site.

Selling Reupholstery

1. Today reupholstery can cost almost as much as a new piece of furniture. It can be completed, however, more quickly than waiting for special order furniture. When considering reupholstery, be sure that:
   A. The sizes are appropriate.
   B. The shape is desirable.
      Note: Additional comfort can be taken care of by reworking the insides of the piece.

2. There seem to be no rules as to what types of fabric can be applied to particular types of furniture today. *Example:* Large floral traditionals are often seen on small occasional chairs.

3. When choosing patterns it is important to pay close attention to pattern match and extra yardage requirements. This is particularly important with plaids. Also note whether fabrics can be railroaded and which direction stripes are to be applied.

4. Workrooms:
   A. Workrooms should be chosen carefully for quality to reach your client's expectation level.
   B. Yardage estimates should be made by workrooms. This should not be the designer's responsibility.
   C. Be sure to give the workroom all information available regarding pattern repeats and application requests before the measurement for proper bidding.
   D. Ballpark bidding can be done by the designer first, but the client must be aware that all figures are subject to final measurement by the workroom. Most furniture catalogs have approximate yardage charts that can be used for general estimating.

5. When problems occur and need to be corrected, follow carefully the steps recommended on page 135 Problem Solving.

Selling Furniture

1. **Do your homework first.**
   A. Complete space planning.
   B. Determine budgetary guidelines.
   C. Determine physical needs.
   When a client expresses "Has to sit-in-it" itis try to discourage this by explaining the following...
      1) As a designer you are qualified to note appropriate measurements of existing furniture and recommended pieces.
      2) There are so many manufacturers and so many pieces that merchants today cannot begin to show all that is available.
      3) They need to trust you - See page 248 on the "Doctor".
      4) When you've sold yourself effectively, the client won't be so picky!
   Note: Client's expectation level. Client preferences. (Note that nothing is perfect - sell the wrinkles!)

2. **Make your first presentation.**
   A. Present the two best options first.
   B. Point out the advantages of your best option.
   C. Keep comparing everything to your first choice.
   D. Note the specific points in your selection such as relationship of: Back Height....... Arm styles......... Seat cushion..........Leg style.
   Different pieces sit differently for different people. The designer must be fully aware of this. When in doubt, seek help from showroom salespeople.
   E. Let them know you've done your homework.
   F. Refer to benefits and value.

3. **Time consuming legwork.**
   A. If your client is undecided and can't clarify their thoughts:
      1) Let them do the running around.
      2) Send them out to do **their** homework.

B. Bring them to showrooms when:
  1) You need to show them a sample of what you are trying to sell.
  2) You need to make them believers:
    a. In the quality you'll sell them.
    b. In all we have access to.
    c. In what you want them to buy.
  3) You need help in selling furniture.
     Pre-work with the showroom people and ask for their help.
C. Let them know you've helped them narrow down all the options to just the right one for their needs.

4. **The closing** should take place by the third appointment or you have not been working your previous appointments as effectively as possible.
  A. Have your paperwork ready. All you need to fill in is their signature.
  B. Carefully review what you are selling.
  C. Pre-sell the wrinkles.
  D. Don't make promises on deadlines and deliveries.
  E. Thank them for their order and their check.
  F. Get excited for them.
  G. Shake hands when they leave.
  H. Compliment them on their good decision making.

5. **Custom designed upholstered furniture** should only be a design option under the following conditions:
  A. To duplicate an existing piece that a client already has.
     Example: A new loveseat to match existing sofa.
  B. When a manufactured piece does not exist in the appropriate style and price range.

  Note: Unless you have very qualified workrooms, you are likely to be heading into very murky water.

Selling Custom

If you call yourself a designer as opposed to a decorator, custom work is the only way to go. Almost every product offers the opportunity for creative custom work. Doing something custom protects you from being "shopped". It gives your client something really special for their money. It will provide endless conversational networking opportunities, for you as well as your client.

Products Which Lend Themselves To Custom Work:

Wallcovering: Handpainting for borders or special areas.
Window Treatments: Soft shades, verticals, draperies,cornice boards, valances, tie backs, etc. Consider handpainting for the ultimate design experience.
Furniture: Coffee tables, sofa tables, etageres, desks,ottomans, chairs, sofas.
Custom Cabinetry: Entertainment centers, storage units.
Mill Work: Moldings, trims, mantels.
Carpeting and Area Rugs: Bordering, custom patterns.

Professional Guidelines When Selling Custom to a Client:

1. **The designer must be totally in control of a custom project.** Do not depend on your client for direction. If you are inexperienced in a particular area, then you must rely totally on the workroom you are using as a resource. Make sure your workrooms are qualified and stand behind their workmanship 100%.
2. **There should be no surprises.** If there are, the designer has not communicated carefully enough with the workroom and the client. The total responsibility lies with the designer. If there is a problem, it is the **designer's** fault.

3. **To eliminate potential problems, consider the following:**
   A. Request strike-offs for approval. (Additional charges are well worth the cost.)
   B. Be realistic about your expectations. Make sure the client is also realistic. Custom does not mean perfect, just like working with a designer does not equal perfection. Remember you too are working with an artisan. If you have confidence in your workroom you need to trust their design discretion also.
   C. Make sure your paperwork and measurements are in perfect order .
   D. It is mandatory to communicate in person with the workroom on a custom order.
   E. Photographs, color swatches, wallcovering and fabric samples are necessary for clear communication.
   F. When it comes to ordering custom upholstered furniture, do so because:
      1) You need to match an existing piece and cannot find a manufacturer who will make it in the correct size and detail therefore it is easier to go custom.
      2) You want to be truly creative and the project budget allows you to do so therefore you can design an original piece. Be sure that the budget is sufficient to allow a full mark up for such a project.
      3) You can actually do it for less money by going custom as opposed to a comparable piece from a major manufacturer.
   G. **Do not order custom upholstered pieces because:**
      1) The client can't find something they like.
      2) The client is fussy about details.
         A client like this is too much in control and will never be satisfied. The designer has not done their homework and they do not know

how to sell the wrinkles properly. You begin the
project by losing money unless you have allowed
for a tremendous profit margin. Ample profit
margin is one way to eliminate this opportunity, or
better yet make money at it.

Last but not least, custom should be done because the
designer has chosen to do so.

Step by Step to Selling "Custom"

1. Think of the **functional needs** of your client.
   A. Listen to them talk.
   B. Ask questions about their needs.

2. By designing something that is functional and yet attractive and unique you have added a very special value to your product which can't be "shopped".
   A. Contract application.
      1) Your specification is unique.
      2) You are doing something "above average"
   B. Residential application
      1) You are designing, not specifying.
      2) You are creating something their friends will talk about.

3. Create the understanding that custom pieces do not always mean higher prices. You need to compare "apples with apples"!

4. Learn how to compare "apples with apples" in products and manufacturers quality. Be as knowledgeable as possible.

5. **Pricing Guidelines**
   A. If you sell value and function in addition to uniqueness you shouldn't have a problem with pricing.
   B. Get a "rough estimate " first before going into a lot of drafting time. A 50% mark-up is the minimum. Remember most furniture is doubled so it is not out of line to do the same for "custom" if pricing is realistic and within the client's budget.
   C. Make rough sketch concepts for initial client approval.
   D. Limit your time in proportion to hours/commission:
   Drafting
   Pricing
   Bidding

E. Staining and Finishing
It is best if this is priced separately and noted that prices are subject to change depending on the final decisions. Many custom finishes require more time than standard colors and stains.

F. Installation Costs
Delivery costs should be included in the finished price. Clients react more positively if this fee is not separated from the total.

G. Lighting/Mirrors/Hardware/Molding
1) Be sure to include all miscellaneous extras that are to be a part of the completed installation.
2) Hardware is easily overlooked. In many situations it is better to exclude and use concealed pulls. This decision should be noted on your contract.
3) Many workrooms do not supply lighting fixtures. It is advisable to work with a good electrician.
4) Molding decisions are very important. Most workrooms have standard catalogs with profile illustrations to facilitate decisions.

6. When the job is sold.....personally deliver and communicate the purchase order with your supplier/ workroom. It is also good to do a final measurement and finishing walk-through at the job site with the client and the workrooms. Double check all communications carefully.

7. Make sure your quote sheet is clear and all expectations are clearly dealt with first. Sell the wrinkles and know what you are going to deliver.

8. Don't forget how you are going to get your product into the room.

Designing Entertainment Centers

Designing custom cabinetry for audio visual needs or entertainment centers is one of the strongest areas in need of good design today. Custom cabinetry is the best way to do the job right. Consider the following:

1. Work with a good showroom that will provide back up knowledge and expertise in the technical areas.

2. Be aware of:
   A. Long range goals and needs of the client.
   B. Lifestyle and income level.
   C. Client's equipment.
      1) VCRs
      2) TVs
      3) Components
      4) Speakers

3. Draw an initial sketch with your concept for the client. Get them excited about your services in this particular area.

4. Show your expertise as a professional designer who keeps up with current trends.

5. Show pictures or take them to available showrooms to lend credibility to your recommendations.

6. Professional audio consultants may charge an hourly rate. However, if they are selling merchandise, this fee may be waived. It is a good idea to have your plans and sketches approved or reviewed by an audio visual consultant if your client is considering new or special merchandise.

7. Recommended viewing distances are as follows:
   A. 27" eye level is best.
   B. 20" Screen......8-12 ft.
   C. 26"-60"Screen...10-15 ft.

8. Give projected costs for a complete entertainment center. Get overall approval before proceeding with more detailed drawings.

9. Once final drawings and pricing have been approved, make sure your workrooms have double checked for areas you may have forgotten and of course, final detailed measurements. Make sure you are using qualified workrooms.

10. Don't forget about:
    A. Cords
    B. Ventilation..(3-4" recommended on all sides)
    C. Liquid areas.....aquariums/bars

11. Finishing: Overall guidance and color recommendations should have been made throughout the designing process. Remember a large entertainment center's color is very important. Strike-offs for approval are essential.

Glossary of Terms in Home Entertainment

Surround Sound: An audio enhancement of videotape which decodes the surrounding sound information provided in the movies. Prerecorded video tapes of these movies include the encoded sound information. New products are needed to decode it for home use. Extra speakers and amplifiers are needed along with the decoder. The Dolby name indicates that the decoder has been approved by Dolby Labs (proprietor of the originating technology.)

Digital: The word itself indicates only quantifying information, however, the term digital is being used for everything from speakers to VCR.

PIP: Picture within a picture. New televisions with digital circuitry can provide small insert pictures within the main picture, so that two video sources - or five - can be watched at the same time. This can be a VCR, a videodisc, or even a security system.

Stereo TV: Usually refers to broadcast television (versus stereo vcrs) which has been standardized by the FCC and is available in most higher priced televisions today. It is being broadcast by more and more television stations.
> MTS-Multi-channel Television Sound. Same as Stereo TV
> SAP-Secondary Audio Program. Incorporated in the FCC standards for stereo TV. Allows two monophonic audio programs to be broadcast at the same time (in two languages, for example.)

Front Projection TV: Large screen television in which the projector which carries the source is in front of the screen. The projector can be floor or ceiling mounted.

Rear Projection TV: A method by which the projector is in back of the screen, in a one piece unit that can often be as narrow as the rest of the system. Screen sizes can go up to around 60" diagonal screens.

Direct View TV: Another name for the traditional cathode ray tube television. New direct view TV's can have up to 35" diagonal screens.

DAT: Digital Audio Tape format for audio. Records music on a very small tape cassette digitally so that noise and hiss are eliminated.

Multi-Room Systems: Allows an entertainment system to be controlled throughout the home from one system.

Subwoofer: A hi-fi term. Since bass sounds are non directional, if the bass is incorporated in a separate box, the loudspeakers for the higher frequencies can be smaller. Subwoofers can be used as coffee tables, with their attendant small speakers placed on shelves, for instance.

Videodisc: A disc that looks like a record that incorporates both audio and video sound that is decoded by a player that uses a laser.

CD: Compact disc. The compact disc player has become an integral part of any home entertainment system. It is an audio product that decodes sound by laserbeam and is digital technology. The records are approximately 4" in diameter. The players are now available in many configurations, ranging from small portables to units that incorporate changers (To play up to 250 CD's at once.)

CDI: Compact disc interactive. A brand new system of incorporating video into compact disc technology and allows random access for interactive functions, such as video games. Standards are being set. This is not on the market.

CD-Rom: (Random Only Memory) An information system using a compact disc instead of a floppy disc with greatly increased storage capability. Basically storing printed matter only.

CD-V: A new system incorporating compact discs and the new compact disc video which plays five minutes of video with digital sound and 20 minutes of pure digital sound.

LCD: Liquid crystal display. Currently being used as the technology for small flat screen televisions. Not available in larger sizes yet.

HQ: High quality. Recent improvement in VHS VCR which produces a better picture.

Superbeta: Improvement on the original Beta VCR which reduces the visual noise to produce a better picture with better duplication properties.

S-VHS: New to VHS, allowing much greater picture definition. However, S-VHS recorded tapes are not compatible with other VHS formats. It requires special wiring between VCR and TV. The TV must have S-VHS inputs to utilize the tape properly.

Remodeling

Recognizing the Need/Opportunity

1. Active Client Listening - When you hear a client discuss the need for remodeling or make comments such as "My office is such a mess" or "I don't have any storage space," begin marketing space planning and remodeling services.
2. Show them pictures from your portfolio and discuss major remodeling projects you have been involved in.
3. Remodeling and the designing of cabinetry offers a designer one of the greatest opportunities to show off their complete design capabilities.

Clarifying Your Role

My favorite quote on remodeling is *"Remodeling is like giving birth to an elephant. It helps to have the zookeeper in attendance."*

1. Decide the best way to work together.
   A. Straight consultation
      An hourly rate for consultation throughout the project is the most lucrative and least stressful way to go.
   B. Overseeing the project
      A flat fee needs to be negotiated for overseeing the project. You would also be advised to have a separate contract with the client as to what services will be rendered for that fee.
   C. General Contracting the project.
      A minimum fee of 15% of the overall project cost is recommended. This usually does not begin to cover the headaches and the time it takes to do the job well. Lien waivers are necessary when acting as the general contractor. (See Lien form) Contact your attorney for complete verification of this process.

No designer should attempt a remodeling project unless under the direction of an experienced resource person.

Initial Walk-Through at Site

1. A designer should get paid for an initial walk through consultation. Begin by discussing needs and coming up with a workable space planning sketch to leave with the client. Discuss the following:

   A. Traffic Patterns
   B. Location of entertainment centers
      1) Audio-visual equipment
      2) Bar, counters, serving area
      3) Gaming areas
   C. Location of work spaces
      1) Computer
      2) Desk
      3) File cabinets
      4) Storage
      5) Laundry
      6) Tool bench
   D. Furniture Layouts
   E. Lighting
   F. Windows/Doors
   G. Additional Rooms/Areas:
      1) Baths
      2) Exercise
   H. Fireplace

Reclarifying Your Role

1. Review your contract with the client.
2. Review the above with the client to decide the best way of working throughout the project, i.e. when you will be charging for time and when you will not be charging for time.

Potential Pitfalls

1. Make the client aware of a realistic budget.
2. Discuss scheduling realistically. Don't make any promises.

3. Discuss the importance of working with a reputable general contractor. A contractor working for a design company on an on-going basis will be more accountable than if hired by a client once.

Remodeling Facts You Should Know

Project	Average Cost	Resale $/%*
Major Kitchen Remodeling	$20,527	70%
Minor Kitchen Remodeling	$ 7,266	78%
Room Additions	$43,131	62%
Bathroom Remodeling	$ 6,369	69%
Adding a Full Bath	$ 9,130	96%
Adding a Fireplace	$ 3,513	94%
Replace Windows, Doors	$10,222	59%
Adding a Skylight	$ 3,335	68%

As you can see, certain remodeling projects add value to your home. Planning a remodeling project effectively begins with:

1. Professional Space Planning
2. Professional Design Services

* The figures above are based on averaging 18 U.S. cities. The entire study is available from Remodeling Magazine, 655 15th St. NW, Suite 475, Washington D.C. 20005 phone: 202-737-0717

Add-Ons

1. Think "add-ons" whenever possible.
   You must be in the client's home frequently to do this.
   You should take careful notes to use at the appropriate time.

2. "Add-on " examples:
   A. Fun foliage $ 50-$500
   B. Picture reframing $100-$300
   C. Throw pillows $ 50-$100
   D. Lamps $150-$550
   E. Accessory/art piece $200-$500

3. The facts:
   A. $50 a day=$18,250 a year: $1,825 extra commission

   B. $100 a day=$36,500 a year: $3,650 extra commission

4. Save one day a week, preferably Friday, to list all the add-ons you can think of that you became aware of this week. Mark one day a week on your calendar for add-ons. You may be able to charge additional hourly rates for your services.

5. To make additional sales and money on add-ons, you must be very organized with your time. This should be done when you are in a particular area and not making a special trip. Remember that time is money and if you are not handling this effectively, doing add-ons is not profitable for you.

Guidelines to Selling Lamp/Shades

1. Never order a single lamp at a time. Freight costs drive the lamp cost up horribly. If not passed on to the client, these extra costs can eat up all profits. It's best to order lamps in groups of six or more.

2. When special ordering a lamp to match an existing lamp (creating a pair), always order two lamps. Matching the first can be a potential problem.

3. When a client is looking for shades only, send them out to find them at stores that specialize in lamp shades. There are too many variables such as width at the top base of the shade, height of the shade, etc. that can cause problems if not perfect. If the client does not wish to do this, perhaps an hourly fee is in order.

4. Lamps can be time-consuming to find. The following is my own personal method.
   A. Request the authority to make new lamp-lighting selections.
   B. Get an overall budget approval.
   C. Take good notes on desired needs/effects:
      1) Height
      2) Color
      3) Finish
      4) Shade tones
   D. Use preferred showrooms and do an initial 1 hour maximum walk-through. Take notes - moving lamps to appropriate positioning on comparable tables, buffets,etc.
   E. Narrow down your options to the winning finalists.
   F. Bring the lamps out to the client's home and properly position them.

5. Let the client try them in their home for 3-4 days.

6. If the client does not wish to keep them:
   A. They should return them to the proper showroom.
   B. Ask them to look on their own.
   C. Do not continue to assist them further unless it is financially worth it because:
      1) They will come with you.
      2) They will pay for your time if they don't purchase the second time around.
      3) The total job size is large enough, $15,000+ to warrant your spending more time.

How To Sell Art

1. Discuss budget first.
   A. Prints - $20-$80 unframed.
   B. Limited Editions/Collectible Prints "$150-800" un-framed.
   C. Framing - from $120 to $250 for a standard una-dorned 25" x 30" piece of art.
   D. Original art costs cover a wide range.

2. Ask for input on preferences or requests. (Ask for adjectives)
   > Landscapes
   > Nature - Oceans/Mountains/Streams
   > People
   > Abstract
   > Impressionistic
   > Realistic

   Most people don't know what they want or what they need. That's why they haven't purchased art. Verbalize for them what you see!

3. Verify appropriate size/shape/subject matter you'll be looking for by noting the focal points of the room. Let them browse through your art files to get an idea of what appeals to them if you need some input.

4. Get a feeling for how involved the client needs to be.
   A. If they need to see the options, pre-select 5-6 pieces and meet them at a showroom.
   B. Better yet - pre-select 2-3 and bring them to their home.

5. If they need several pieces of art for one room only, pre-select the key piece first. Bring 2-3 options for adjacent areas.

6. Don't get into framing options until the picture is 85% sold.
   (Framing should be a separate topic.)

7. Determine your role as the art authority. The client needs to be aware that you will charge for your time if purchases are not made through you, unless you love giving your time and expertise for nothing!

8. Know when to close. If it's right for the client's budget and their room: **CLOSE IT!**

Framing

1. The simpler the better is a good rule of thumb. You are framing the piece of art, not the room. Don't make the frame more important than the art.

2. Choose your main mat color first. Select a color from within the piece of art itself for the main mat color. Use the color in the center of the art if possible.

3. Double & triple mats should be the same color saturation.

4. Framing should accentuate the art.
   A. It's wrong if you feel a clash.
   B. Whites should be close to the art white.
   C. Fillets are good for more traditional art. Antique jeweled inserts are also good.

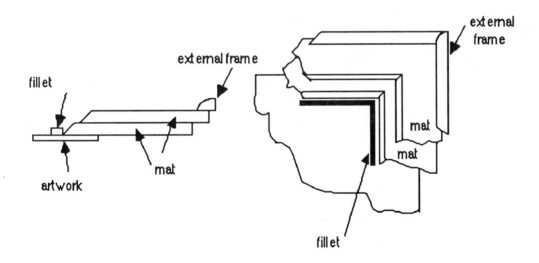

5. Inner mat colors should contrast with art.
   A. Dark art: light inner mat.
   B. Light art: dark inner mat.
   C. Triple mats: dark-medium-light dimensions must vary.

6. The bottom margin should be wider than the top margin.
7. If the art paper is beautiful, it is often advisable to float the art in order to see the edges.
8. Size: Little pieces can be framed large. This is best done vertically.

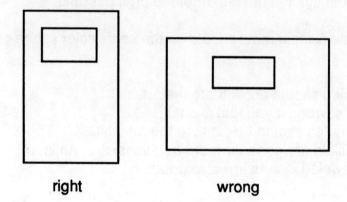

right   wrong

Fabric Cleaning Codes

These are standards in the home furnishings industry. A good general rule is when spills occur, blot immediately with an absorbent towel, never rubbing the spot.

Code "S" cleaning instructions:
Professional dry-cleaning is recommended. **Clean this fabric with pure solvents only**, and be cautioned that using water-based or detergent-based cleaners may cause water stains or excessive shrinking. The water stains may become permanent and unable to be removed with solvent cleaning agents. To prevent overall soil, frequent vacuuming or light brushing to remove dust and grime is recommended.

Code "SW" cleaning instructions:
Professional dry-cleaning is recommended. **Clean this fabric with water-based cleaning agents, foam, or pure solvents.** To prevent overall soil, frequent vacuuming or light brushing to remove dust and grime is recommended.

Code "W" cleaning instructions:
Professional dry-cleaning is recommended. **Clean this fabric with water-based agents or foam** to remove overall soil, and be cautioned that many cleaning agents are harmful to the color and life of fabric. To prevent overall soil, frequent vacuuming or light brushing to remove dust and grime is recommended.

Code "X" cleaning instructions:
Clean this fabric only by vacuuming or light brushing to prevent accumulation of soil. Be cautioned that water-based foam or solvent-based cleaning agents of any kind may cause excessive shrinking or fading.

System 11: *Marketing*

Sizing Up Your Prospect

A good friend of mine once asked me a simple question: "Who's your customer?" I answered him by saying, "Eden Prairie (name of suburb) people in a middle income bracket!"

"No, really," he continued, "who is your customer?"

I knew I was getting into trouble now because every answer I continued to give him just didn't satisfy him. He wanted specific details such as: age, group, sex, income level, occupational patterns: retired, self-employed, part-time, full time professionals, blue collar workers; marital status; family averages; home information; rented vs. owned, and so forth. What surprised me most was how little I knew about my customer, my potential prospect.

"How do you really know who to market yourself to," he said, "if you don't really know who your prospect is? You can bet your competition knows! They spend billions of dollars gathering this information."

I've been paying a lot closer attention to the simple question of who is your client....therefore, who is your prospect? The following are some guidelines I've uncovered along the way in my quest to discover who my client is.

1. **Don't prejudge a potential prospect.** (Leave that to amateurs!) Ask significant questions to discover: who they are, their needs and personality. If you have a computer, create client profile sheets and start tabulating this information.

2. Take a good, hard look at what you are really selling and who you:
   A. **Can** sell it to.
   B. **Want** to sell it to.

3. Take a good, hard look at your **business image**. Is it compatible with who you really want to sell to? What is your competition doing better?

4. **How do you expect to reach your prospect?**

   If you answer this one by saying something like, "word of mouth and referrals have always been just great for me," then you really have no intention of growing. Business people that stay in business and grow, know how to promote, continually.

5. Become acutely aware of the timing element when prospecting:

   A. **When the prospect is in a hurry.** Make a definite appointment for another time.
   B. **When your prospect is worried.** Set up another date to see them.
   C. **When they are tired.** Schedule appointments when they are "fresh" and alert - on their best time not yours!
   D. **When they are preoccupied.** See your prospect when you are apt to get full attention. Lunch and breakfast meetings can be excellent.

6. Become sensitive to your prospects buying and behavioral patterns:

   A. **The uncommunicative customer.** Talk slowly, treat them with real courtesy, smile a lot, win their confidence with facts, stress quality, be enthusiastic.
   B. **The impulsive buyer.** Don't waste time with details, don't oversell, don't let their mind drift, go for emotions.
   C. **The meditative or deliberate buyer.** Slow down, give all the needed facts and small details, constantly ask them if they have any questions, be ready to spend a longer time with this client, paint vivid pictures.

D. **The buddy-buddy buyer.** Watch out for their built in charm to overpower you, don't be out maneuvered, use their charm to your advantage to keep control.

E. **The egotistical buyer.** Never argue a point, flatter them and allow them to be the expert, let them make the decisions and compliment them for making decisions quickly, be very diplomatic, give your views only as if they are suggestions, keep building their ego.

F. **The hesitant or undecided buyer.** Give them many minor decisions as opposed to any major decisions.

7. **Be an excellent listener.** Note the choice of the word excellent. "Good" is just not good enough today!

Sizing up your prospect is really part of "working smarter not harder". Become a professional and learn to think on your feet. Only then will you start to see the fruits of your labor and pains.

Advertising

"To advertise" or "not to advertise". So often I hear business owners talk about how they do not advertise. They are so busy they do not need to advertise. I'm often tempted to ask:

1. How much do you actually make a year? ($15,000 or $50,000?)
2. What is your gross margin? (20% or 40%?)
3. How many hours do you average for a $10,000 sale? (2 hours or 20?)

This book is about becoming more successful. It is about making a living at interior design. If you plan to be financially successful, advertising is essential.

There are many inexpensive ways to advertise. Referrals are the **best**. Approximately 60% of my clientele comes from referrals. Some of the best forms of advertising are "low - no cost" forms of advertising.

Advertising Suggestions:

1. **Networking**: Daily - Weekly - Monthly - Yearly.

2. **Customer Servicing**
   A. Satisfy your customers - They are your best advertising.
   B. If a problem arises, handle it promptly and professionally - a client who has had a problem which has not been solved satisfactorily, can provide the worst kind of advertising.
   C. It cost six times as much to acquire a new customer as it does to retain an old customer. With this in mind, perhaps you should take half of your current advertising budget and put it into customer relations and services.
   D. It takes far less time and money to service and negotiate a WIN-WIN settlement with a client than to hire an attorney or go to small claims court.

3. **Promoting Yourself in Local Newspapers/ Newsletters**

You should learn to write your own press releases and take photos whenever appropriate. Our company is committed to having one press release in a newspaper every month. Get to personally know the people at the newspaper office. It works and it costs nothing. People are always commenting on how often they read about us in the paper.

We also advertise regularly in our local newspaper. We have learned that if we expect to get frequent press releases we must be regular advertisers. Remember the old "I'll scratch your back if you scratch my back" theory. It works.

4. **Quality advertisements do make a difference**

We have learned it is worth the difference to hire a professional ad layout person rather than to expect a newspaper staff person to design a quality ad. **You get what you pay for**, if you are careful.

A. Advertising dollars that don't create sales are wasted dollars. Buying an ad in a newspaper that covers a 150 mile radius is an expensive way to reach potential customers if people will only drive 30 miles for your type of product or service.
B. Effective advertising is directed to a specific person. You need to know who it is you are trying to reach and how best to reach them.
C. Look at your advertisements. The focus on the customer should outweigh emphasis on you by at least two to one. Your buyer wants to know how they will benefit by the money spent.
D. How much should you spend on advertising? There is no magic formula. Review your ads for the last 12 to 18 months and determine why one particular ad or form of advertising out-performed

the others. Use this information to decide what advertising to do and how much to spend in the future.

We advertise in a upscale health club magazine targeted specifically to our clientele - the monthly cost is approximately $100 and is well worth the exposure we get to over 12,000 people.

Kate Halverson
Owner

5. **A Business Newsletter**

This has been an excellent form of advertising. Each newsletter has promoted us in the following ways:

A. Sharing exceptional design stories with photographs. Clients love to share their stories and it's a good way for them to promote us among their friends. Others look for the opportunity to have their stories shared.
B. Inviting them to upcoming events. This is a great opportunity for vertical networking.
C. Educating clients to all your services. On the job, residentially and commercially.
D. Sharing inside information indicating company resources.
E. Personalizing with Designer Columns or recipes.

The newsletter is a controlled chance to say what and who you are. Clients have been known to keep their newsletters on file for many months before calling for their first appointment. Our mailings have been up to three times a year with mailing lists of up to 3,300. This gets expensive and you need to analyze the return and scale the expensive to the size of your business.

6. **Direct Mail**

   A. If you haven't used direct mail, perhaps you should consider doing so. Reasons for using direct mail:
      - You can mail to a very specific list.
      - You can send different offers to different people.
      - You can test one offer against another by splitting your mailer to different lists.
      - You can use lots of photos and lots of ad copy.
      - You can test offers to small lists rather inexpensively.
   B. Your best mailing list is from your customer files.
   C. You can rent lists for targeted markets.
   D. You can't contact your customers too often. They will appreciate receiving advance notice of events and special promotions.

7. **A Design Brochure**

The brochure is usually given or mailed, along with the newsletter, to any potential client. Using the brochure checklist with a customer in their home on the first call is a great tool for discussion of services.

The brochure is very effective when networking and prospecting. Leave it in a very visible place for clients to browse through when waiting. Sometimes real estate or condominium lobbies are excellent places to leave a brochure.

8. Portfolio

Have a working portfolio of completed projects with both residential and commercial clients. It is a very effective tool for prospective clients.

Photographs . . . . . before and after shots are great! You can use a Polaroid for before shots but good after shots must be professionally done.

9. Letters of Reference

You should obtain letters of reference, especially on business letterhead, whenever possible. To facilitate this, you can help by writing the letter or suggested points for the client to include on their own letterhead. See sample reference letters on page 204 and 324.

10. Business Cards

All designers and design consultants should use business cards. Business cards say a lot about your business image and your name brand identity. Examine many options before you decide which image you want to project. Make sure it looks professional and successful.

11. Direct Mail Catalogs

This is the age of the direct mail order catalogs and 1-800 numbers. For a custom interior design business it just makes the competition tougher. Learn to separate yourselves from the mass merchandisers and capitalize on custom work. Forge a nitch that cannot be shopped. Learn from your competitors. They make it very easy customers and that is why they are so successful. Do you make it easy for your clients?

My two years of involvement with franchising the design business taught me a lot of lessons:

a. One of our major competitors is hamburgers. Look at what a great job they do just to sell cheap hamburgers. How well do you think people expect to be treated when purchasing a big ticket design product? Ten times better or 1,000? Can't you understand why?
b. Franchises are successful because they have professional consistent systems - Do you?
c. We have lots to learn by observing what franchises are doing. If you want to compete with franchise businesses, you must learn from them. If you choose not to, target a different market, but be sure you know who your market is.

FOR IMMEDIATE RELEASE

Contact:
Date:

The Historical Society recently completed their new offices, located in the former City Hall Building. The new quarters provide space for display cases and conference seating along with built-in cabinetry for record storage. Mary Gullickson, a contract designer with Touch of Class Interiors, Ltd., worked with the Society members on their project. The colors used in flooring, window treatments, furniture and wallcoverings were pulled from different antiques the society has collected through the years.

PHOTO

FOR IMMEDIATE RELEASE

Contact:
Date:

Kate Halverson, owner of Touch of Class Interiors, has been been a featured speaker for several area functions this past month. She participated in a panel discussion for the Women's Forum at the Small Business Expo. She also spoke at International Market Square's ICON '89.

Halverson will be continuing her speaking tour with Window Fashions Magazine as they hold seminars across the country.

Sample Newsletter

Interiors you want to stay HOME for!

Think of TOC for:
- Kitchen Planning Services
- Bathroom Planning Services
- Remodeling Services
- Space-Planning
- Consultation Only
- All Interior related products
  - Carpeting-Flooring   Furniture
  - Window Treatments   Accessorizing

Kate Halverson
President, Touch of Class Interiors

I've always said that the sign of a well designed interior is when you and your guests feel so comfortable . . . they don't want to leave. Another way of saying it is having a home so comfortable, you look forward to always coming home.

TOC specializes in comfortable ideas . . . creative ideas . . . at comfortable prices. Call us today with your questions and concerns about working with a design firm.

Festival of Trees
Nov. 19-22
The Conservatory at 8th and Nicollet

Visit The Festival of Trees where Designer Trees will be featured and available for sale. Touch of Class will feature a very special tree entitled . . . A Touch of Class! . . . what else?

PROGRAMS with a *Touch of Class*
- for your club
- for your firm
- for your church
- for your friends . . .

Catering Services may be included

Call Elizabeth at 941-3023 for further information

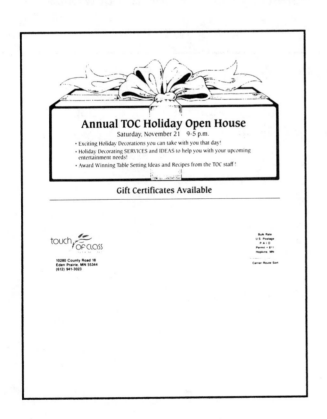

Annual TOC Holiday Open House
Saturday, November 21   9-5 p.m.

- Exciting Holiday Decorations you can take with you that day!
- Holiday Decorating SERVICES and IDEAS to help you with your upcoming entertainment needs!
- Award Winning Table Setting Ideas and Recipes from the TOC staff!

Gift Certificates Available

touch OF CLASS

10280 County Road 18
Eden Prairie, MN 55344
(612) 941-3023

Sample Reference Letter - Residential

Nothing speaks more highly of your services than a good letter of recommendation from a satisfied client. You will want to ask your client as a normal part of the "closing procedure".

Here is an example of a reference letter we received:

Dear Designer:

I would like to take this opportunity to thank you for all your hard work on our project and let you know how pleased we are with how it looks.

Each room has the "feel" that we discussed. By using creativity, you were able to keep the budget close to what we had in mind.

We also appreciate the support we had from everyone at your studio. Again, thank you for all your work and the attitude that you weren't just working for us, but with us.

Sincerely,

Note: We sometimes find it less of an imposition if we have a client fill out a Client Review Form (page 169) instead of writing a letter of recommendation, it depends on the scope of the project.

Networking

I didn't realize until a few years ago that I was brought up networking. My father was a minister and my mother was the perfect minister's wife. Everyday was filled with:

- Meeting new people.
- Making people feel good about themselves.
- Helping people solve problems.

My mother never waited for others to offer their hand in introduction. She always offered her hand first and:

- Made a quick introduction
- Gave a short comment as to her affiliation/position
- Turned the conversation to the other person with an open ended question
- Tried to establish a trust relationship

She did this all naturally! It wasn't until several designers on my staff attended various functions with the express purpose of networking, that I realized they didn't have the necessary skills to do it. Here are some guidelines to help to improve your networking skills.

Networking continually needs nurturing. Past clients, present clients, and potential future clients continually need attention. We all need nurturing, like seeds ready to sprout, flowers ready to bloom. The funnel system (explained on page 332) continually needs to be fed. That's why fifteen years later, once a week I still dedicate one day a week to long range planning and public relations.

Wednesday's are dedicated to:

1. Having networking lunches with potential clients.
2. Inviting specific persons the visit the studio to learn what we are all about.
3. Calling former clients and catching up on their past year and present design needs. See the tickler system on page 333.

4. Taking time to work on future projects and business concerns or promotional activities.

It's true - continual networking is the funnel system and the funnel system truly does prevent potential problems. If you are not actively funneling new work in and keeping contact with former clients, your well will soon dry up because someone else will be doing a better job. Keep in contact with people on a four to six week basis. A short note or a phone call is all that is needed. Make sure there is some kind of contact on a regular basis so that they remember who you are.

It has been said that it costs six times as much to acquire a new customer as it does to retain an old customer. With this in mind, perhaps you should take half (yes, half) of your current advertising budget and put into customer relations and services.

Getting yourself motivated on a daily basis isn't easy . . . it takes work and discipline! Getting yourself motivated when sales are down is especially difficult. Here are some thoughts to clip and save for those extra lean months which will inevitably confront you some time in business.

1. Focus on the "up" people. Ask them how they keep so positive all of the time. Just talking to a positive mentor will be helpful. No doubt you will learn that you are not alone and that life does bring drought periods but plentiful rains will follow eventually.

2. Find a good quote to post and focus on. A couple of my favorites are:

"The will to persevere is often the difference between failure and success."
David Sarnoff

"The harder I work, the better my luck."

Ed Bradley, CBS News

3. Fill slow times with effective networking. Vertical and horizontal network weekly. This means not just being satisfied by telling your story to a person, (horizontal networking), but ask that person to network for you too, (vertical networking). Polish "telling your story". Telling your story is being able to give your business an effective, enthusiastic, one minute commercial at the instant an opportunity arises.

Example:
   "Hi, I'm Kate Halverson, owner of Touch of Class Interiors in Eden Prairie. We're a full service design studio for both home and business interors. We specialize in custom work."

A. Tell your story
B. Be good to people.

Telling your story is sharing what you do, where you do it and how good you are at it. Experience, of course, makes this all easier. Being good to people is as old as the golden rule. Thinking about how you have been treated by other businesses and how you'd like to be treated is just common sense.

The following is a list of places to look for clients:

1. Social organizations
2. Professional and civic groups
3. Church groups
4. Friends and family
5. Public speaking opportunities...(adult education, women's groups)
6. Prospecting...cold calls to non-competing businesses
7. Referrals from present clients

8. Employees
9. Directories (college, high school, businesses, suburbs)
10. City, government and county records...(building permits, new households, marriage licenses, property tax lists)
11. Newspapers...(ads and leads)
12. Mailing lists...(faculties etc.)
13. Interprofessionals: Architects, engineers, and other professionals in design - related fields are excellent sources for clients. They often have jobs that need interior design services.
14. Contractors: Both general contractors and sub-contractors work on projects which may have opportunities for a design professional.
15. Manufacturers, representatives, wholesalers, suppliers, distributors: All salespeople in the field are aware of future projects.
16. Owners of large buildings: Are sources to learn about new clients in either office or apartment buildings.

You must stay in touch with any person or firm you truly wish to build a strong networking system with.

Develop a "tickler" system where you note every 4-6 weeks who should be called back and why.

Devote at least one day a week to networking.

Follow these guidelines for successful networking:

1. **Meet business contacts on a regular basis.**
   Go to seminars, workshops, meetings - any kind of an organized program. Plan events and situations to occur on an average of every four to six weeks throughout the year. You'll find that at almost any community meeting you end up speaking with new people or renewing an acquaintance which will lead to more useful conversation.

2. **Network with your competitors.**
   There are many good ways to share information
   without jeopardizing your business.

I wish I had a dollar for all the networking events I've
been at over the years. Networking or "working a room"
effectively is work - unless you are focused on your
overall purpose - the event can often seem like a waste
of time and money. Take the time to pre-think your
overall purpose in attending. Ask yourself the following:
- Are you going just for fun?
- Are you going to meet new people?
- Are you going to meet potential new clients?

Your socializing skills will need to be focused if you
intend to meet potential clients.

**Here are some other tips for networking at business
events:**

- Rehearse a quick eight to ten word description of your
  business.
- If someone sounds interested, take their card and
  promise to call the next day. A networking event is
  not the time for an hour long sales call, it's for brief
  chats.

10 Rules of Networking

1. **Get out of your Cocoon.** Socialize. Pick out a spot in a group and move into it. Start listening. After a few minutes try the basic introductory steps. Do not be afraid to say 'hello' to someone. People are usually flattered that you have taken the time to talk to them.

2. **Set Goals for Yourself.** What kinds of people do you need to meet? How many contacts do you need to make? Someone once said you should "tell your story to 5 people daily, belly to belly." How did you do at the last professional meeting you attended? How did you do this week?

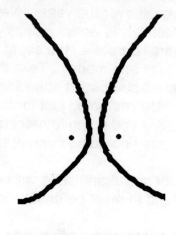

3. **Trade Information.** Exchange ideas, experiences, contacts. Tell them who you are, but also listen to who they are. Be a resource. "I know where you can get that."

4. **Play Host.** Ask someone if they are enjoying the meeting. Introduce someone to another person in the room who might be a good contact for them.
   Example:
   "Do you know Jack Nelson, he's an excellent installer. He's sitting over there in the blue jacket. I'd be glad to introduce you if you'd like."

5. **Set up Follow-up Appointments**. Make the contact first, then follow up by inviting a key contact to lunch or to your place of business.

6. **Make Friends.** Learn what you have in common. Let them ask for your business card. Don't hustle. Attitude is the key. You need to be outgoing and fun.

7. **Learn to relate to others.** Forget your own needs for the moment. Lock into others dreams and aspirations. Your own rewards come by helping others, not by climbing over them.

8. **Ask for what you need**. Find the person who can provide it. If you don't ask, you don't get and you don't learn. People really feel good when helping others out.

9. **Keep digging.** Broaden your base. Make as many contacts as you can. Go deep when it makes sense. You can never know too many people.

10. **Remember:** The more you give, the more you get. Always help others whenever you can.

Good networking contacts do not happen overnight and it is not easy work. Networking professionally will build credibility and contact which will prove to be mutually beneficial for years to come.

The Funnel System

It is easy to relax when business is good. It is easy to feel comfortable after several years in the business and consider networking as something "For Beginners Only". It is easy to become overconfident with success and just plain forget about networking. I've felt that way several times in my design career only to be brought to reality over and over again realizing that a successful business-person, a true professional can never forget - **THE FUNNEL SYSTEM:** The dots represent clients. There should be clients at every stage of the chart. The only satisfied client is one that comes back or sends a referral that buys.

Contributed by Basil Wissner

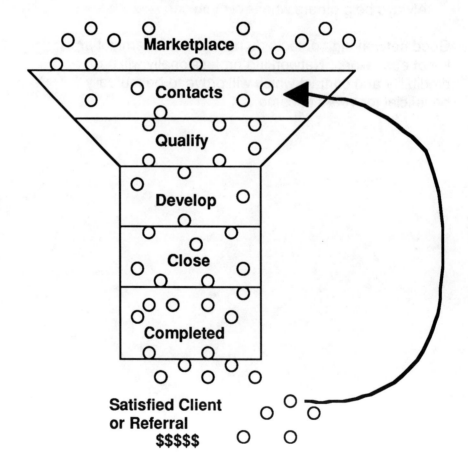

Marketplace

Contacts

Qualify

Develop

Close

Completed

**Satisfied Client
or Referral
$$$$$**

The Tickler System

I first heard about a "Tickler File" from my attorney. He explained that for every client he has a special card completed. Here's our version:

```
Follow Up Form

Possible Additional Work:
Rooms:
Possible Needs:
Approximate date to call back:
Designer:
Date:
```

When a project is complete, the card should be filled out noting potential work for the future. Almost every house has further opportunities for design work. I, however, might not seek to do more work with a client due to:

1. Their personality
2. Their unrealistic budget
3. Lack of design challenge

If, I wish to have their repeat business as well as their friends and business associates, the tickler card is completed and placed in the appropriate month's file. My tickler box is near my desk. At the beginning of each month I pull out all the cards for the month and vow to call each and every client. It is a wonderful system. My clients really feel flattered that I have taken the time to check up on them. Sometimes I do find out about things I wish I didn't know, such as faded wallcovering they'd like me to replace. Old problems I've learned to handle as "the cost of doing business" or "general advertising and promotional costs". In most cases it just doesn't arise or they really don't expect you to do anything.

The tickler file is for networking and promoting the funnel system. It does work! I wish I'd started it sooner.

Keeping Clients

Taking good care of your clients, listening to their needs, and being professional is all part of keeping clients. Don't forget the following guidelines:

1. Use the **personal** wherever possible. Show that you care about them, their family and their pets. . . . whatever is important to them is important to you.

2. Work continually on repeat orders or phases two and three. Call back regularly like a dentist does...showing that you care. Log careful notes in your calendar or prospect file.

3. **Don't let down with your clients.** Always keep a positive mental attitude. Don't bore them or let them get involved with your personal problems.

4. Always be aware of their true needs; if you don't know what they are, ask questions until you do. This is your most important job. Often they won't tell you the truth straight out. You have to dig for it!

5. **Be fun**. Use a little showmanship. Act like a pro!

6. Always be aware of your appearance. Be neat and classy.

7. Keep a log of important dates in your clients' lives. Send cards when appropriate.

8. Always make your client feel important and special.

9. Act confident and successful. Business is always good! Success breeds success.

10. Remember to say "thank you" . **Show appreciation** ...always!

Marketing Checklist for Retailers

This list is for small retailers and covers customer analysis, buying, pricing, management and promotion. You can use it to evaluate your interior business, to evaluate your current status and to possibly rethink certain decisions.

Customer Analysis

Who are your target customers and what are they seeking from you?

1. Have you profiled your customers by age, income, education, occupation, etc.?
2. Should you try to appeal to the entire market rather than a segment(s)?
3. Are you familiar with your customer's lifestyles?
4. Are there new customer segments or special markets that deserve attention?
5. Have you looked into possible changes taking place among your target customers which could significantly affect your business?
6. Do you know where your customers live?
7. Do you use census data from your city or state?
8. Are you aware of the reasons why customers would buy from you? (Convenience, price, quality products, etc.)
9. Do you stress a special area of appeal such as better quality, wider selection, convenient location, or convenient hours?
10. Do you ask your customers for suggestions on ways to improve your operation?
11. Do you know what products or services your customers most prefer?
12. Do you belong to a trade association or local Chamber of Commerce?
13. Do you subscribe to important trade publications?
14. Do you know what seasons and holidays most influence your customers buying behavior?

15. Have you considered using a consumer question-naire to aid you in determining customer needs?
16. Do you know at what other types of stores your customers shop?
17. Do you visit market shows and conventions to help anticipate customer wants?

If you have a retail storefront operation, consider the following:

1. Have you a merchandise budget (planned purchases) for each season?
2. Does it take into consideration planned sales, planned stockturn, and planned markdowns?
3. Have you broken it down by departments and merchandise classifications?
4. Have you a formal plan for deciding what to buy and from whom?
5. Have you identified areas of negotiation that allow you favorable terms for buying (payment terms, promotions assistance, transportation costs, special buys, etc.)
6. Have you identified all internal and external sources of market information available?
7. Have you a system for reviewing and testing new items coming onto the market?
8. Have you considered using a basic stock list or a model stock plan in your buying?
9. Are you using either a unit or dollar merchandise control system?
10. Do you keep track of the success of your buying decisions in previous years to aid you in next year's buying?
11. Do you attempt to consolidate your purchases with several key suppliers?
12. Does your buying reflect an improved return on investment?
13. Do you plan exclusive or private brand programs?

14. Do you take advantage of cash discounts and allowances offered by your vendor/supplier?
15. Do you have reasonable expectations from your vendor?
16. Does your vendor have reasonable expectations of you?
17. Have you developed a trusting relationship with your vendor/supplier?
18. Have you a useful vendor/supplier evaluation system for determining their performance?

Pricing

Have you established a set of pricing policies and goals?

1. Have you determined whether to price below, at, or above the market?
2. Do you set specific markups for each product?
3. Do you set markups for product categories?
4. Do you use a one-price policy rather than bargain with customers?
5. Do you offer discounts for quantity purchases, or to special groups?
6. Do you set prices to cover full costs on every sale?
7. Do the prices you have established earn the gross
8. Do you clearly understand the market forces affecting your pricing methods?
9. Do you know which products are slow movers and which are fast?
10. Do you take this into consideration when pricing?
11. Do you experiment with odd or even price endings to increase your sales?
12. Do you know which products are price sensitive to your customers, that is, when a slight increase in price will lead to a big dropoff in demand?
13. Do you know which of your products draw people when put on sale?

14. Do you know the maximum price customers will pay for certain products?
15. If the prices on some products are dropped too low, do buyers hesitate?
16. Is there a specific time of year when your competitors have sales?
17. Do your customers expect sales at certain times?
18. Have you developed a markdown policy?
19. Do you take markdowns on a regular basis, or as needed?
20. Are you influenced by competitors' price changes?

Promotion

Are you familiar with the strengths and weaknesses of various promotional methods?

1. Are the unique appeals of your business reflected in the store image? (quality product, special services, etc.)
2. Are these appeals promoted on a consistent basis?
3. Have you considered how various media and promotional methods might be used for your firm?
4. Do you know when it is profitable to use institutional advertising?
5. Do you know when product advertising is better?
6. Can you make use of direct mail?
7. Do you have a mailing list? If so, has it been updated recently?
8. Do you participate in activities of your Chamber of Commerce, Merchants' Association, Better Business Bureau, or other civic organizations?

Is there financial or technical assistance available which you can use to enhance your promotional efforts?

1. Have you considered customer seminars and classes?

2. Can you get help from local newspapers, radio, or television?
3. Are cooperative advertising funds available from vendor/suppliers?
4. Do you ask customers to refer your business to friends and relatives?
5. Do you make use of community projects or publicity?
6. Would a newsletter be useful to contact customers or remind them of your store?
7. Do you study the advertising of other successful retail firms, as well as of your competitors?

Are your products displayed to maximize their appeal within the store?

1. Do you know which of your items have unusual eye appeal and can be effective in displays?
2. Are you making use of window displays to attract customers?
3. Have you a schedule for changing various displays?
4. Do you display attention - getting items where they will call attention to other products as well?
5. Do you use signs to aid your customers' shopping?
6. Do signs in your store provide useful price and product information?
7. Do you know which items are bought on "impulse" and therefore should be placed in high traffic areas?
8. Do you have an attractive storefront?

Management

Have you developed a set of plans for the year's operations?

1. Do your plans address changing consumer markets and lifestyles?
2. Do your plans provide methods to deal with competition?
3. Do your plans address market potential?

4. Do they contain creative approaches to solving problems?
5. Do they include financial requirements?
6. Are they realistic?
7. Are they stated in such a way that you know when they have been achieved?
8. Is there a system for auditing your objectives?
9. Have you a formal plan for setting aside money to meet any quarterly tax payments?

Are you organized effectively?

1. Have you thought about the long-term direction of your business?
2. Are job descriptions and authority for responsibilities clearly stated?
3. Does your organizational structure minimize duplication of effort and maximize the use of each employee's skills?
4. Do employees understand how they will be rated for promotion and salary increases?
5. Would you or some of your employees profit by taking business education courses offered at local schools/colleges?
6. Will training help your employees achieve better results?
7. Do you use positive personal leadership techniques like being impartial, giving words of encouragement and congratulations, and listening to complaints?
8. Do you avoid all forms of discrimination in your employment practices?
9. Do you have a formal program for motivating employees?
10. Have you taken steps to minimize shoplifting and internal theft?

Have you an effective system for communicating with employees?

1. Do you hold regular meetings that include all personnel?
2. Do your employees have their own bulletin board for both material you need to post and items of general interest?
3. Have the "rules and regulations" been explained to each employee?
4. Does each employee have a written copy?
5. Is each employee familiar with other positions and departments?
6. Do you have an "open door" policy in your office?

Operations and Special Services

Do you know what type of credit program (if any) you should offer?

1. Does the nature of your operation require some type of credit for your customers?
2. Have you discussed credit operations with your local credit bureau?
3. Would a credit program be a good sales tool?
4. Have you looked into other programs of credit cards?
5. If you set up your own credit program, do you know what standards you should use in determining which customers can receive credit for what item periods and in what amounts?
6. Do you know all of the costs involved?
7. Will the interest you charge pay for these costs?
8. Are you familiar with the Truth-in-Lending legislation?

Have you adequate insurance coverage?

1. Do you have up-to-date fire coverage on both your building equipment and inventory?

2. Does your liability insurance cover bodily injuries as well as such problems as libel and slander suits?

3. Are you familiar with your obligations to employees under both common law and workers' compensation?
4. Has your insurance agent shown you how you can cut premiums in areas like fleet automobile coverage, proper classification of employees under workers' compensation, and by cutting back on seasonal inventory insurance?
5. Have you looked into other insurance coverage, such as business interruption insurance or criminal insurance?
6. Do you have some fringe benefit insurance for your employees (group life, group health, or retirement insurance) ?

Do you offer any special customers services?

1. Do you provide personal services for your customers?
2. Do you provide time saving services for greater customer convenience?
3. Do you charge for delivery?
4. Have you thought about using a commercial delivery service?
5. If not, do you know how to work the delivery expenses into the selling price of your products?
6. Have you selected competent and professional personnel to provide customer services?
7. Have you a policy for handling merchandise returned by customers?
8. Are your services purchased on a routine contractual basis?
9. Do you make use of gift services?
10. Are your prices for services competitive?
11. Do you measure the quality of your services through customer surveys or other methods?

Financial Analysis and Control

Have you established a useful accounting system?

1. Do you know the minimum amount of records you need for good control?
2. Do you know all the records you should keep in order to meet your tax obligations on time?

Do your sales records give you the key information you need to make sound decisions?

1. Do you have a cash flow plan or budget?
2. Can you separate cash sales from charge sales?
3. Can sales be broken down by department?
4. Can they be broken down by merchandise classification?
5. Do they provide a way to assess each salesperson's performance?

Do your inventory records give you the key information you need to make sound decisions?

1. Do they show how much you have invested in merchandise without the necessity of a physical inventory?
2. Have you achieved the optimum balance between inventory and cash?
3. If you hold too much inventory, are you aware of the additional costs?
4. Do you know the difference between inventory valuation at cost and at market?
5. Would a computer ease your inventory control procedures?
6. Do you understand the pros and cons of the costs method of inventory accounting versus the retail method?
7. Have you found an accounting method that shows the amount of inventory shortages in a year?

8. Are you aware of inventory - related costs such as pilferage, obsolescence and spoilage?

Do your expense records give you key information you need to make sound decisions?

1. Do you know which expense items you have the greatest control over?
2. Are the records sufficiently detailed to identify where the money goes?
3. Can you detect those expenses not necessary to the successful operation of your business?

Do you effectively use the information on your profit and loss statement and balance sheet?

1. Do you analyze monthly financial statements?
2. Can you interpret your financial statements in terms of how you did last year and whether you met this year's goals?
3. Do your financial statements compare favorably with other similar businesses in terms of sales, cost of sales, and expense?
4. Are you undercapitalized?
5. Have you borrowed more than you can easily pay back out of profits?
6. Can you see ways to improve your profit position by improving your gross margin?
7. Have you forecasted financial statements for future growth?

These questions are meant to help you analyze your retail operation from the marketing viewpoint. You should know the strengths of your business and products. You must also know the real problems you are up against. Your business depends on your good sense and management foresight. You must adapt to new markets, product changes, and be innovative to keep your business growing.

Adapted from: U.S. Small Business Administration: **Marketing Checklist for Small Retailers**, by Michael W. Little.

Interior Design Myths

People already have many built-in ideas and opinions concerning the interior design business. It is our ongoing job to work at breaking down any existing barriers.

- Be aware of the following stereotypes.

- Educate potential clientele wherever possible.

- Always try to project a warm, professional and friendly personality.

The following myths and stereotypes seem to be most common in our business:

Myth #1 **Using an Interior Designer will cost you more money.**

Wrong, a professional designer will help you spend your decorating dollars more wisely. An interior designer is like a good travel agent. A travel agent helps prepare you for a trip. The trip costs no more because you used a travel agent. Often times, it will cost you less. The same holds true for a designer.

Myth #2 **The designer makes all the decisions.**

Wrong, the designer just narrows down the options. You make the final decisions! We're the "House Doctor" that still makes home visits and helps you eliminate your household aches and pains.

Myth #3 **Designers throw out everything.**

Wrong. Good designers always work around quality or special existing pieces.

If they choose to use consultation time only - remind them of the "Permanent Solution".

One hour of design consultation costs approximately the same amount as a permanent wave and a haircut. A permanent wave usually lasts no longer than three months. A consultation should give you lasting options for your money - permanent solutions.

Consumer Presentations

Another way to promote yourself is to make interior design presentations to the public. Here are some ideas for areas on which you can speak.

DESIGN RELATED TOPICS

Cocooning - Building Your Interior Nest
Decorating - Where Do I Start?
Accessorizing with a "Touch of Class"
Space Planning - Where Do I Start?
Giving Your Home/Office a Facelift
Personalized Decorating
Art: How To Buy It/How To Hang It
Remodeling - To Do Or Not To Do!
Decorating For The Holidays
Working With A Designer - Why You Can't Afford Not To
Window Winners: Function vs. Flair
The Eclectic Look - How To Pull It Off
Color My Home Beautiful - Trends and Changes
Design Trends for the Future
How to Buy Furniture With Confidence
Buying "Custom" - and Still Meeting Your Budget

Sample Biography

It is important to start and keep current a biographical listing of your design-related accomplishments. This can be used in your portfolio or at appropriate presentations. It really becomes a more professional updated resume. It can be used when someone is introducing you for programs. If you are just starting out, add you firm's accomplishments to the list. Most owners would be happy to enhance your biography. Here are some suggested categories to cover:

1. Experience
   - Design
   - Administration
   - Technical
   - Communication
2. Education
3. Publications
4. Awards
5. Travel

Experience	Reference
Complete kitchen renovation design and installation services.	H. D. Lange Residence Plymouth, MN
New construction consultation for 4,500 sq. ft. residence and design implementation.	P. L. Smith Residence Des Plains, OH
Design consultant and specification for 35-unit hotel.	Dennison, NY
Technical Skills	
Designed built-in cabinetry and audio environment center for residential application.	C. H. Nelson Residence New Hope, PA

Experience

Designed fireplace addition and custom cabinetry wall for townhouse residents.

Space planned 1800 sq. ft. great room addition for client.

Reference

P. R. Lewison
Residence
Prairie View, OK

L. D. Hanson
Residence
Bloomville, MA

Education

BA degree from:_____

2 year degree from:_____

References

(List at least three.)

Professional Affiliations

Allied Member of ASID (American Society of Interior Designers)
Member of IFDA (International Furnishings and Design Association)
Chamber of Commerce

Marketing for Realty Firms

Realtors provide a great resource for referrals. Plan to select two to four area realty firms that are in close proximity to your design studio. Consider those firms with the best local reputations. Meet with the manager personally and request an opportunity to make a presentation at one of their weekly staff meetings.

1. **Introduction**
   A. Introduce yourself, company and services offered.
   B. Bring appropriate portfolios and literature.
   C. Immediately dispel myths concerning the use of a designer.

2. **Specific Services Offered for Realtors/New Home Buyers:**
   A. Consultations for Buyer
      1) Provide remodeling budget expertise
      2) Provide decorating budget expertise
      3) Provide unbiased home comparison critique
      4) Provide creative, thought provoking ideas
      5) Special servicing contact/referral for out of town purchaser
   B. Consultations for Seller
      1) Updating color schemes
      2) Spaciousness "tricks of the trade"
      3) Smoothing out the rough edges
   C. Presentations for Current Buyers
      1) Dear "New Home Owner"
      2) Services and Products

3. **Referral Fee Program for Realtor**
   Develop a referral fee system for new clients received from realtors.
   A. $50.00 cash to the realtor for a $5,000+ job.
   B. One hour free consultation for referral to be used by realtor or realtor's client. Have the realty firm visited make a copy of the information handout sheets they want.

Note: List realty firms and office managers visited on a master copy with the owner. This avoids any duplication by various designers within a firm.

Sample Letter to Condo & Townhouse Owners

Dear Condominium or Townhouse Owner:

Selecting and purchasing a condo is an exciting and important decision. At _____, we appreciate the importance of good decision making. We specialize in servicing this often overwhelming process when it comes to your interiors as well as designing for your lifestyle.

We would like to offer you two special opportunities:

1. One complimentary planning consultation for your condo (One hour - value $_____) - no charge

    or

2. An informative seminar for your condo association members on one of the following topics: (minimum six to a group)

    Combining "Old" with New
    Accessorizing for a Finished Look
    Maximizing Interior Spaces

Call today for an appointment or stop by our studio to discuss your needs. The time is now for you to add a "touch of class" to your exciting condominium.

Sincerely,

Sample Builder's Package

The builder's package has been put together to facilitate ongoing working relationships with builders. This package shows professionalism in addition to concern for the builder's needs. A designer must become a team player and a time saver. In order to build a strong referral program with a builder, the key would be to:

1. **Fill a need**
2. **Make the builder look good**

Here are some points to use in self-promotion with builders.

1. **Packaging** is assuming a major role in selling homes. If the floor plan is adequate, but the decorating wasn't done very well compared to the competition, people probably wouldn't buy the house.

2. **Decorating** a home superior to the house price range makes the house look even better.

3. Working within a **budget** is important.

4. Working with designers who **listen** is important.

Builder Letter of Introduction

The following is a sample letter to send to all builders in your area. Your builders survey should also be included. The personal touch is always better than a letter so be sure and prescreen those you send to and follow up with a phone call after you've sent your package. You will never get any response without continued follow-up.

Dear Builder:

Enclosed is some information about our studio and our services. We are a full service design studio and are capable of handling the needs of both your company and your home buyers.

We would appreciate the opportunity to talk with you to further discuss our services and ways in which we might work together.

Thank you for your interest in our firm.

Sincerely,

Survey For Builders

If you are interested in doing work with builders or being referred directly to builders you might also consider doing model homes. They are considered by many to be a very good source for referrals and a display for work.

The following is a list of questions you might consider asking a builder. I've learned that it helps to plan what you need to know before making a sales pitch on your services. Not all builders are interested in working with designers. Many feel they have qualified wives. Do your homework carefully.

Do you decorate models?

Are you involved in the Spring Preview or Parade of Homes?

Do you use a professional design service?
Which firm?

Have you been happy with the service you've been using?
Why or why not?

How do you determine the budget for doing your model homes?

Why haven't you used a professional design service?

Has your company ever won a Model Award?

Are you interested in promoting your business by offering design services?

We are interested in learning how you feel about models. Thank you for taking the time to fill out our questionnaire.

Would you be interested in learning more about our Builder's Program?

Yes___No___
Name:
Company:
Address:
Phone:

Building and Selling a "Smart House"

Here are some ideas to have your prospective builder consider:

1. Creating curb appeal at the onset.

2. Selecting a professional merchandiser/designer to help facilitate increased sales.

3. Designing interiors - to accentuate the architectural features of a house.
   Fireplace   Built-ins
   Windows   Porches
   Sun Rooms   Greenhouses
   Balconies

4. Space planning for today's needs:
   A. Home Offices
   B. Audio-Environment Centers/Media Rooms
   C. Gathering Rooms - for cooking, eating and relaxing
   D. Kitchen Suites

5. Lighting expertise to make your home exceptional - not the expected.

6. Woodwork colors - can you mix more than one look in a house?

7. Kitchen cabinetry options - a new look with the warmth of tradition!

8. Storage needs - designing and packaging it into your home.

9. Making wiser, simpler flooring decisions - narrowing down the options successfully.

Fee Options For Builders

Consultation Services Only
1. Model Merchandising
2. Space Planning Review
3. Product Specification and Architectural Design Assistance.
4. Paint, Finishes, Counters, Fireplaces and Other Surfaces
   FEE:
   Consultation services are based on the size of the home/project. A minimum fee is $___ (for x hours consultation time.) (Time can be handled in two or three separate appointments.)

Client Product Selection Assistance

1. Professional interior design services will be provided to the home buyer including the timely review and selection of flooring (carpet, vinyl, tile, hardwood), paint, finishes, tile, fixtures and laminates.
   FEE:
   $___ (for x hours of consultation time). We recommend that the builder include the appropriate amount in the home price and offer the design service as a sales incentive.

2. We will provide all flooring selections and installations for the builder. There will be a base grade offered with upgrades according to the builder's specifications. Installation will be coordinated by our firm.
   NO FEE:
   Interior design service will be provided at no cost when flooring purchases are made through our firm.

> **The Referral System**
>
> For every new home owner/client you refer to our firm we will credit your account:
>
> **___ hours of free consultation time _____ Value**
>
> "There is a big difference between people in an organization working together and all of them just working at the same time. We believe in building a **strong team**."

Product Specification Sheet

Product & Description	Showroom	Allowance
__ Acoustical Walls, Ceiling		
__ Appliances		
__ Bathroom/Plumbing Fixtures		
__ Built In Intercoms		
__ Ceiling Treatments		
__ Counters/Counter Tops		
__ Doors		
__ Entertainment Systems		
__ Fireplaces, Mantels		
__ Floorcoverings/Finishes (Granite, Marble, Brick, Tile, Carpet)		
__ Glass/Windows		
__ Hardware		
__ Kitchen & Bath Cabinetry & Design		
__ Lighting		
__ Mirrors		
__ Skylights		
__ Wall Treatments		

Total Spent:

Notes/Comments:

Model Home Contract

From:
To:

Job Site:
Foreman:
Additional Contractors:

Model Budget:
Completion Date:
Contractual Requirements:

Model Design Statement:

Product/Installation Services Requested:

Additional Design Responsibilities expected:

We require:
1. __% deposit at the onset of the project.
2. __% deposit with order placement.
3. Final payment within ___ days of model completion.

Note: All communications and purchase orders can be approved if authorized by one of the applicable principals.

Any additional design fees that are unforeseen at this time, will be agreed upon prior to billing. Any agreed upon design services which are unforeseen or beyond the scope of this agreement will be billable on an hourly basis.

Builder   **Designer**   **Date**

_____   _____   _____

Leasing Package

Here are a few examples of how you could work with a leasing agent:

1. Be an additional supportive sales tool for leasing agents.
2. Provide professional design services to the tenant.
3. Ease the tenant's decision making process .
4. Prevent unnecessary scheduling problems and delays.

Consultation Only Services

We will assist with the following needs:
Space-Planning
Concept Planning and Selections
Color guidelines as they relate to flooring, wallcoverings, window treatments, furniture selections, and artwork.

The minimum design fee is $___ for __ hours of consultation for the above services. We recommend that the leasing firm include the above amount in the rental package and offer the design service as a sales incentive. Additional hours can be incurred by the client or the leasing agent at a rate of $___ an hour.

Product/Material Specification and Design Implementation Services

We will assist the client in the following selections: flooring, wallcoverings, window treatments, furniture, cabinetry , work stations and accessorizing. We will assist in order placement of the above and installation services required to complete the above.

Hourly rates for consultations will not be incurred by either the leasing firm or the tenant if an initial contract has been signed by the tenant specifying that purchases will be made through our firm. A $_____ minimum order will be required.

Building Allowance Package

We will work within allowance packages if requested by the leasing firm.   Design fees will be charged when purchases are not made through our firm. Ordering and installation services will not be provided by our firm, unless requested by a leasing firm. Procurement fees may be necessary depending on the contractual agreements determined between all parties.

The Bottom Line

Plan Your Work-

Work Your Plan!

This book, **Systems For Success** - has been my plan. The book is intended only to be a framework for building a successful business.

The rest is up to you-

KMH

Recommended Reading List

Communicate Like A Pro.
        Nido Qubein. Prentice-Hall, Inc., 1983.
Complete Professional Salesman.
        Robert L. & Herbert M. Shook. Barnes and
        Noble Books, 1975.
Contact: The First Four Minutes.
        Leonard & Natalie Zunin. Ballantine, 1973.
The Customer is Key.
        Milind M. Lele. John Wiley & Sones, 1987.
Get The Best From Yourself.
        Nido Qubein. Prentice-Hall, Inc., 1983.
Guide To Business Principles and Practices for the Interior Designer.
         Harry Siegel. Whitney Library of Design,
        1982.
How To Profit in Contract Design.
        Andrew Loebelson. Interior Design Books,
        1983.
How to Turn Customer Service into Customer Sales.
        NTC Business Books, 1988.
How to Win Customers and Keep Them for Life.
        Michael LeBoeuf, Ph.D. G. Putnam's Sons,
        1987.
In Search of Excellence.
        Thomas Peters & Robert Waterman.
        Harper & Row, 1982.
Interior Design Business Handbook, The.
        Mary Knackstedt, Whitney Library of
        Design, 1988
Listening: The Forgotten Skill.
        Madelyn Burleyl-Allen. John Wiley & Sons,
        1982.
Megatrends.
        John Naisbett. Warner Books, 1982.
Networking - The Great New Way for Women to Get Ahead.
        Mary Scott-Welch. Warner Paperback,
        1983.

Personal Organization; The Key to Managing Your Time and Your Life
        Harold Taylor.
Professional Selling Techniques.
        Nido Qubein. Prentice-Hall, Inc.1983.

Prospering Woman.
        Ruth Ross. Whatever Publishing, 1982.
Quality is Free
        Philip Crosby. McGraw-Hill, 1979.
Service America!.
        Karl Albrecht and Ron Zemke. Dow Jones-Irwin, 1985.
Shut Up and Sell! Tested Techniques for Closing the Sale.
        Don Sheehan. Amacom, 1981.
Talking Straight, Assertion Without Aggression.
        Ronald Adler. Holt, Rinehart & Winston, 1977.
Women and Work - Honest Answers to Real Questions.
        Carole Hyatt. Warner Paperback, 1980.
You Can Negotiate Anything - How to Get What You Want.
        Herb Cohen. Lyle Stuart, 1980.

Index

Quick Index to Forms

Authors and Titles Cited

ORDER FORM

Send ____ copies of **Systems for Success** $39.95 U.S. + $2.50 shipping per book.
(Minnesota residents add 6%)

(Inquire regarding quanity discounts)
372 pgs./8.5 x 11/Illustrated
Indexed for easy reference
ISBN 0-9623401-1-1
LC 89-51681

Featuring new, improved, flexible OTABIND binding - bound to stay open.

Your Name_____

Firm Name_____

Address_____

City_____State_____Zip_____

Phone #_____

Payment:
- check
- Visa/MC:
    Card #_____exp. date:___
    Signature:_____

Thank you for your order.
Allow 3-4 weeks for delivery.

Weston Communications
10280 County Road 18
Eden Prairie, MN 55347
612/941-3090